Books are to be returned on or before
the last date below.

THE SUNDAY TIMES

How to Manage People

Michael Armstrong

KoganPage

LONDON PHILADELPHIA NEW DELHI

Publisher's note

Every possible effort has been made to ensure that the information contained in this book is accurate at the time of going to press, and the publishers and authors cannot accept responsibility for any errors or omissions, however caused. No responsibility for loss or damage occasioned to any person acting, or refraining from action, as a result of the material in this publication can be accepted by the editor, the publisher or the author.

First published in Great Britain and the United States in 2008 by Kogan Page Limited
Reissued 2011
Reprinted 2009, 2010, 2012

120 Pentonville Road   525 South 4th Street, #241   4737/23 Ansari Road
London N1 9JN   Philadelphia PA 19147   Daryaganj
United Kingdom   USA   New Delhi 110002
www.koganpage.com   India

ISBN   978 0 7494 6163 8
E-ISBN   978 0 7494 6164 5

The views expressed in this book are those of the author, and are not necessarily the same as those of Times Newspapers Ltd.

British Library Cataloguing in Publication Data

A CIP record for this book is available from the British Library.

Library of Congress Cataloging-in-Publication Data

Armstrong, Michael, 1928-
    How to manage people / Michael Armstrong.
        p. cm.
    Includes bibliographical references and index.
    ISBN 978-0-7494-6163-8 -- ISBN 978-0-7494-6164-5 (ebk) 1. Management--Handbooks, manuals, etc. 2. Leadership--Handbooks, manuals, etc. I. Title.
    HD38.15.A765 2011
    658.3--dc22
                                                        2010024017

Typeset by Jean Cussons Typesetting, Diss, Norfolk
Printed and bound in India by Replika Press Pvt Ltd

Contents

Introduction

The aim of this book is to give practical advice to managers and team leaders on how to manage people in their teams – getting the best results from them and dealing with any people problems that may arise.

It is often said that people leave their managers not their organizations. This may not always be true but there is something in it. So far as many people are concerned their manager is the organization. They do not have much contact with other people in authority. A business may have all sorts of progressive HR policies but it is managers who have to make them work on the ground.

Managers depend on their people. They cannot do without their wholehearted commitment and support. But gaining that support, motivating and engaging them and ensuring that they know what they are expected to do and how to do it is down to managers. And it is a difficult task. This book is designed to make it easier by going into the main actions that managers have to carry out to get things done through people, namely: managing effectively overall, leading, motivating, team building, delegating, interviewing, managing performance, developing and rewarding people, managing change and handling people problems.

The book focuses on what frontline managers, ie those directly controlling teams of people, have to do themselves. Of course, many organizations have HR specialists to give advice and help. But managers have largely to do it themselves. As Professor John Purcell of Warwick University says: 'It's managers who bring HR policies to life.' And many managers have to do their job without HR advice and this book is particularly designed to meet their needs.

1

What managers do

As a manager you are there to get things done through people.
You are engaged in a purposeful activity involving others. But you
are concerned with defining ends as well as gaining them. You
decide what to do and then ensure that it gets done with the help
of the members of your team. You deal with programmes,
processes, events and eventualities. All this is done through the
exercise of leadership.

People are the most important resource available to you as a
manager. It is through this resource that other resources are
managed. However, you are ultimately accountable for the
management of all resources, including your own. When dealing
with immediate issues, anticipating problems, responding to
demands or even a crisis, and developing new ways of doing
things, you are personally involved. You manage yourself as well
as other people. You cannot delegate everything. You frequently
have to rely on your own resources to get things done. These
resources include skill, know-how, competencies, time, and
reserves of resilience and determination. You will get support,
advice and assistance from your own staff and specialists,

including HR (human resources), but in the last analysis you are on your own.

The rest of this book examines particular aspects of managing people, such as leadership, organizing and motivation. This chapter focuses more generally on what you need to be and do to exercise your people management responsibilities effectively. It starts with an overall look at the criteria for managerial effectiveness. This is followed by a review of the attributes of effective managers. The rest of the chapter deals with a number of the key aspects of management.

Managerial effectiveness

As a manager and a leader you will be judged not only on the results you have achieved but the level of competence you have attained and applied in getting those results. Competence is about knowledge and skills – what people need to know and be able to do to carry out their work well.

You will also be judged on how you do your work – how you behave in using your knowledge and skills. These are often described as 'behavioural competencies' and can be defined as those aspects of behaviour that lead to effective performance. They refer to the personal characteristics that people bring to their work roles in such areas as leadership, team working, flexibility and communication.

Many organizations have developed competency frameworks which define what they believe to be the key competencies required for success. Such frameworks are used to inform decisions on selection, management development and promotion. Importantly, they can provide the headings under which the performance of managers and other staff is assessed. Managers who want to get on need to know what the framework is and the types of behaviour expected of them in each of the areas it covers.

The following is an example of a competency framework:

- *Achievement orientation.* The desire to get things done well and the ability to set and meet challenging goals, create own measures of excellence and constantly seek ways of improving performance.
- *Business awareness.* The capacity continually to identify and explore business opportunities, to understand the business priorities of the organization and constantly to seek methods of ensuring that the organization becomes more business-like.
- *Communication.* The ability to communicate clearly and persuasively, orally or in writing.
- *Customer focus.* The exercise of unceasing care in looking after the interests of external and internal customers to ensure that their wants, needs and expectations are met or exceeded.
- *Developing others.* The desire and capacity to foster the development of members of his or her team, providing feedback, support, encouragement and coaching.
- *Flexibility.* The ability to adapt to and work effectively in different situations and to carry out a variety of tasks.
- *Leadership.* The capacity to inspire individuals to give of their best to achieve a desired result and to maintain effective relationships with individuals and the team as a whole.
- *Planning.* The ability to decide on courses of action, ensuring that the resources required to implement the action will be available and scheduling the programme of work required to achieve a defined end-result.
- *Problem solving.* The capacity to analyse situations, diagnose problems, identify the key issues, establish and evaluate alternative courses of action and produce a logical, practical and acceptable solution.
- *Teamwork.* The ability to work cooperatively and flexibly with other members of the team with a full understanding of the role to be played as a team member.

Some organizations illustrate their competency frameworks with examples of positive or negative indicators of behaviour under each heading. These provide a useful checklist for managers willing to measure their own performance in order to develop their careers. Table 1.1 is an extract from a framework used by a large housing association.

Table 1.1   Positive and negative indicators of performance

	Manage performance **Do things well and achieve the objectives and standards** **agreed for the role**
Positive indicators	• Carries out work as required • Completes work on time • Meets quality/service standards • Works accurately • Sees things through • Asks for ground rules • Committed to achieving high-quality results • Shows commitment to make it happen • Seeks to raise quality standards • Puts measures in place • Actions match words • Takes ownership of things to be done • Evaluates and revises deadlines as necessary • Takes responsibility for outcomes • Always has a follow-up course of action • Makes contingency plans • Does everything within their means to ensure that things get done to the best of their ability • Confronts issues
Negative indicators	• Frequently forgets things • Has to be chased to meet deadlines • Not concerned with quality • Does not learn from mistakes • Does not follow instructions

- Often late in delivering expected results
- Work not up to standard
- Makes too many mistakes
- Does minimum they can get away with
- Relies on others to complete actions
- No pride in the job
- Blames others for personal failure
- Conceals situations when things go wrong
- Focuses on less important activities
- Builds achievements to be greater than they are
- Agrees unrealistic deadlines
- Prioritizes badly

Attributes of successful managers

Michael Pedler and his colleagues suggest, on the basis of their research, that there are 11 attributes or qualities which are possessed by successful managers:

1 Command of basic facts
2 Relevant professional knowledge
3 Continuing sensitivity to events
4 Analytical, problem-solving and decision/judgement-making skills
5 Social skills and abilities
6 Emotional resilience
7 Proactivity
8 Creativity
9 Mental agility
10 Balanced learning habits and skills
11 Self-knowledge

Key aspects of management

The following key aspects of management are examined in the rest of this chapter:

- exercising authority;
- making things happen;
- prioritizing;
- exercising control;
- problem-solving;
- being decisive.

Exercising authority

Authoritative people are listened to. They get things done and others take note of what they say and act on it. Good managers demonstrate that they are authoritative by the way they behave. They rely on the authority of expertise and wisdom rather than the authority of power. Managers may be 'drest in a little brief authority' but they have to earn respect for that authority and keep on earning it. Ten things to do if you want to be authoritative are set out below.

Being authoritative – 10 things to do

1. Be good at what you are doing as a leader, a manager, an expert or all three.
2. Be able to define clearly what you expect people to do clearly, concisely and persuasively.
3. Demonstrate that you know where you are going, what you are doing and why you are doing it.
4. As necessary, explain the course of action you are taking.
5. Lead by example.

6. Accept that your authority is not absolute – it only exists if others recognize it.
7. Be decisive but avoid rushing into decisions without careful thought.
8. Get people to accept that there will be occasions when what you say goes – you are accountable and the final decision is always yours.
9. Be self-confident and convey that to everyone concerned.
10. Be a good communicator, ensuring that people know exactly what is expected of them.

Making things happen

Making things happen, managing for results, getting things done – this is what management is all about. Managers have to be achievers, taking personal responsibility for reaching objectives. John Harvey-Jones, in *Making it Happen*, said of the approaches used by successful business managers:

- Nothing will happen unless everyone down the line knows what they are trying to achieve and gives of their best to achieve it.
- The whole of business is taking an acceptable risk.
- The process of deciding where you take the business is an opportunity to involve others, which actually forms the motive power that will make it happen.

How to make it happen: basic questions

It is said that there are three sorts of managers: those who make things happen, those who watch things happening, and those who don't know what is happening. Before finding out how to get into the first category, there are three questions to answer:

1. Is making things happen simply a matter of personality
   – characteristics like drive, decisiveness, leadership,
   ambition, a high level of achievement motivation – which
   some people have and others haven't?
2. And if you haven't got the drive, decisiveness and so forth
   that it takes, is there anything you can do about it?
3. To what extent is an ability to get things done a matter of
   using techniques which can be learnt and developed?

The significance of personality

Personality is important. Unless you have willpower and
drive nothing will happen. But remember that your personality is
a function of both nature and nurture. You may be born with
genes that influence certain characteristics of your behaviour,
but upbringing, education, training and, above all, experience
develop you into the person you are.

Doing something about it

We may not be able to change our personality, which,
according to Freud, is formed in the first few years of life. But we
can develop and adapt it by consciously learning from our
experience and analysing other people's behaviour.

Using techniques

Techniques for achieving results such as setting objectives,
planning, organizing, delegating, motivating and monitoring
performance can be learnt. But these techniques are only as
effective as the person who uses them. They must be applied in
the right way and in the right circumstances. And you still have to
use your experience to select the right technique and your
personality to make it work.

What makes achievers tick?

People who make things happen have high levels of
achievement motivation – a drive to get something done for the
sheer satisfaction of achieving it. David McClelland of Harvard

University identified through his research three needs which he believed were key factors in motivating managers. These were:

1. the need for achievement;
2. the need for power (having control and influence over people);
3. the need for affiliation (to be accepted by others).

All effective managers need to have each of these needs to a certain degree but by far the most important is achievement. This is what counts, and achievers, according to McClelland, have these characteristics:

- **They set themselves realistic but achievable goals with some 'stretch' built in. They prefer situations they can influence rather than those that are governed by chance.**
- **They are more concerned with knowing that they have done well than with the rewards that success brings.**
- **They get their rewards from their accomplishment rather than from money or praise. This does not mean that high achievers reject money, which can in fact motivate them as long as it is seen as a realistic measure of their performance.**
- **High achievers are most effective in situations where they can get ahead by their own efforts.**

10 things high achievers do

1. They define to themselves and others precisely what needs to be done and continually monitor their own performance and that of their team so that any deviation can be corrected in good time.
2. They set demanding but not unattainable timescales and deadlines to do it, which they meet.

3. They are single-minded about getting where they want to go, showing perseverance and determination in the face of adversity.
4. They demand high performance from themselves and equally expect high performance from everyone else.
5. They work hard and well under pressure; in fact, it brings out the best in them.
6. They tend to be dissatisfied with the status quo.
7. They are never completely satisfied with their own performance and continually question themselves.
8. They snap out of setbacks and quickly regroup their forces and ideas.
9. They are enthusiastic about the task and convey their enthusiasm to others.
10. They are decisive in that they are able quickly to sum up situations, define alternative courses of action, determine the preferred course, and convey to the members of their team what needs to be done.

Prioritizing

The sudden and often conflicting demands made on your time means that you will be constantly faced with decisions on when you or members of your team should do things. You will often be in a situation where you have to cope with conflicting priorities. This can be stressful unless you adopt the systematic six-stage approach as described below.

The 6-stage approach to prioritization

1. List all the things you have to do. These can be
   classified into three groups:
   - regular duties such as submitting a report, calling
     on customers, carrying out a performance review;
   - special requests from managers, colleagues,
     customers, clients, suppliers etc delivered orally, by
     telephone, letter or e-mail;
   - self-generated work such as preparing proposals on
     a new procedure.
2. Classify each item on the list according to:
   - the significance of the task to be done in terms of its
     impact on your work (and reputation) and on the
     results achieved by the organization, your team or
     anyone else involved;
   - the importance of the person requesting the work
     or expecting you to deliver something – less
     significant tasks may well be put higher on the
     priority list if they are set by the chief executive or a
     key client;
   - the urgency of the tasks – deadlines, what will
     happen if they are not completed on time;
   - any scope there may be for extending deadlines
   - altering start and finish times and dates;
   - how long each task will take to complete – noting
     any required or imposed starting and completion
     times which cannot be changed.
3. Assess how much time you have available to complete
   the tasks, apart from the routine work which you must
   get done. Also assess what resources, such as your own
   staff, are available to get the work done.
4. Draw up a provisional list of priorities by reference to
   the criteria of significance, importance and urgency
   listed at 2) above.

5. Assess the possibility of fitting this prioritized schedule of work into the time available. If this proves difficult, put self-imposed priorities on a back-burner and concentrate on the significant tasks. Negotiate delayed completion or delivery times where you believe this is possible and, if successful, move the task down the priority list.
6. Finalize the list of priorities and schedule the work you have to do (or you have to get others to do) accordingly.

Described step by step like this, prioritization looks like a formidable task. But experienced managers go through all these stages almost unconsciously, albeit systematically, whenever they are confronted with a large workload or conflicting priorities. What many people do is simply write out a 'things to do' list at the beginning of the week or, in their minds, quickly run through all the considerations described in the above six-stage sequence and make notes on a piece of paper.

Exercising control

You exercise control of activities and the people who carry them out in order to ensure that your plans succeed. But you also need to protect the plans as far as possible from the impact of Murphy's two laws: if anything can go wrong it will; and of the things that can't go wrong, some will. Good control happens when you carry out the following 10 steps.

10 steps to achieve good control

1. Plan what you aim to achieve.
2. Set appropriate and fair targets, budgets and standards.
3. Decide what you want to control.
4. Set success criteria (key performance indicators).
5. Decide how you are going to measure performance.
6. Ensure that measurements are as accurate, valid and reliable as possible.
7. Measure regularly what has been achieved.
8. Ensure that those responsible for results measure their own performance or are provided with measurements that enable them to do so.
9. Compare actual achievements as measured with plans and ensure that every other member of your team does the same.
10. Take or initiate action to exploit opportunities revealed by this information or to correct deviations from the plan.

Problem solving

The process of management, not least the management of people, attracts problems as the sparks fly upwards. At the end of a hard day – and how often they happen – managers can reasonably quote the mantra ODTAA (after John Masefield's book referring to one damn thing after another). However, all is not lost. There are methods of problem solving as given below that can help to overcome the pressure. And you can always seek consolation from a very different type of writer – Karl Marx – who claimed that: 'Mankind always sets itself such problems as it can solve; since, looking at the matter more closely, it will always be found that the task arises only when the material conditions for its solution already exist or are at last in the process of formation.'

10 steps for effective problem solving

1. *Define the situation* – establish what has gone wrong or is about to go wrong – a problem defined is a problem half-solved. And this is the difficult half. The rest should follow quite naturally if an analytical approach is adopted.

2. *Specify objectives* – define what is to be achieved now or in the future to deal with an actual or potential problem or a change in circumstances.

3. *Develop hypotheses* – develop hypotheses about what has caused the problem.

4. *Get the facts* – find out what has actually happened and contrast this with an assessment of what ought to have happened. Try to understand the attitudes and motivation of those concerned. Remember that people will see what has happened in terms of their own position and feelings (their framework of reference). Obtain information about internal or external constraints that affect the situation.

5. *Analyse the facts* – determine what is relevant and what is irrelevant. Diagnose the likely cause or causes of the problem. Do not be tempted to focus on symptoms rather than root causes. Test any assumptions. Dig into what lies behind the problem.

6. *Identify possible courses of action* – spell out what each involves.

7. *Evaluate alternative courses of action* – assess the extent to which they are likely to achieve the objectives, the cost of implementation, any practical difficulties that might emerge and the possible reactions of stakeholders.

8. *Weigh and decide* – determine which alternative is likely to result in the most practical and acceptable solution to the problem. This is often a balanced judgement.
9. *Plan implementation* – timetable, project management, resources required.
10. *Implement* – monitor progress and evaluate success. Remember that a problem has not been solved until the decision has been implemented. Always work out the solution to a problem with implementation in mind.

Being decisive

Good managers are decisive. They can quickly size up a situation and reach the right conclusion about what should be done about it. To say of someone 'He or she is decisive' is praise indeed as long as it is understood that the decisions are effective. To be decisive it is first necessary to know something about the decision-making process as summarized below.

Peter Drucker once wrote:

> A decision is a judgement. It is a choice between alternatives. It is rarely a choice between right and wrong. It is best a choice between almost right and probably wrong – but much more often a choice between two courses of action neither of which is probably more nearly right than the other.

When discussing the solution to problems with people, you should not expect or even welcome a bland consensus view. The best decisions emerge from conflicting viewpoints. This is Drucker's first law of decision making: 'One does not make a decision without disagreements.' You can benefit from a clash of opinion to prevent people falling into the trap of starting with the conclusion and then looking for the facts that support it.

10 approaches to being decisive

1. *Make decisions faster* – Jack Welch, when heading General Electric, used to say: 'In today's lightning paced environment, you don't have time to think about things. Don't sit on decisions. Empty that in-basket so that you are free to search out new opportunities…. Don't sit still. Anybody sitting still, you are going to guarantee they're going to get their legs knocked from under them.'

2. *Avoid procrastination* – it is easy to put an e-mail demanding a decision into the 'too difficult' section of your actual or mental in-tray. Avoid the temptation to fill your time with trivial tasks so that the evil moment when you have to address the issue is postponed. Make a start. Once you have got going, you can deal with the unpleasant task of making a decision in stages. A challenge often becomes easier once we have started dealing with it. Having spent five minutes on it we don't want to feel it was wasted so we carry on and complete the job.

3. *Expect the unexpected* – you are then in the frame of mind needed to respond decisively to a new situation.

4. *Think before you act* – this could be a recipe for delay but decisive people use their analytical ability to come to swift conclusions about the nature of the situation and what should be done about it.

5. *Be careful about assumptions* – we have a tendency to leap to conclusions and seize on assumptions that support our case and ignore the facts that might contradict it.

6. *Learn from the past* – build on your experience in decision making; what approaches work best. But don't rely too much on precedents. Situations change. The right decision last time could well be the wrong one now.

7. *Be systematic* – adopt a rigorous problem-solving approach as described above.

8. *Talk it through* – before you make a significant decision talk it through with someone who is likely to disagree so that any challenge they make can be taken into account (but you have to canvass opinion swiftly).

9. *Leave time to think it over* – swift decision making is highly desirable but you must avoid knee-jerk reactions. Pause, if only for a few minutes, to allow yourself time to think through the decision you propose to make. And confirm that it is logical and fully justified.

10. *Consider the potential consequences* – McKinsey call this 'consequence management'. Every decision has a consequence, sometimes unintended, and you should consider very carefully what that might be and how you will manage it. When making a decision it is a good idea to start from where you mean to end – define the end-result and then work out the steps needed to achieve it.

2

Leadership

As a manager of people your role is to ensure that the members of your team give of their best to achieve a desired result. In other words you are a leader – you set the direction and ensure that people follow you.

It is necessary to distinguish between management and leadership:

- **Management is concerned with achieving results by obtaining, deploying, using and controlling all the resources required, namely people, money, facilities, plant and equipment, information and knowledge.**
- **Leadership focuses on the most important resource, people. It is the process of developing and communicating a vision for the future, motivating people and gaining their engagement.**

The distinction is important. Management is mainly about the provision, utilization and control of resources. But where people are involved it is impossible to deliver results without providing effective leadership. It is not enough to be a good manager of resources, you also have to be a good leader of people.

John Kotter (1991) distinguishes between leaders and managers as shown in Table 2.1.

Table 2.1   Managers and leaders: John Kotter

Management involves:	Leadership involves:
• Focusing on managing complexity by planning and budgeting with the aim of producing orderly results, not change.	• Focusing on producing change by developing a vision for the future along with strategies for bringing about the changes needed to achieve that vision.
• Developing the capacity to achieve plans by creating an organization structure and staffing it – developing human systems that can implement plans as precisely and efficiently as possible.	• Aligning people by communicating the new direction and creating coalitions that understand the vision and are committed to is achievement.
• Ensuring plan accomplishment by controlling and problem-solving – formally and informally comparing results to the plan, identifying deviations and then planning and organizing to solve the problems.	• Using motivation to energize people, not by pushing them in the right direction as control mechanisms do, but by satisfying basic human needs for achievement, a sense of belonging, recognition, self-esteem, a feeling of control over one's life and the ability to live up to one's ideals.

To be an effective leader you need to:

- **understand what is involved in the process – the practice of leadership;**

- **be aware of the different styles of leadership available;**
- **appreciate the qualities that contribute to good leadership;**
- **know how best to develop your leadership abilities.**

These four requirements are discussed in turn in this chapter, which ends with three checklists on leadership.

What leadership involves

Leaders have three essential roles. They have to:

1. *Define the task* – they make it quite clear what the group is expected to do.
2. *Achieve the task* – that is why the group exists. Leaders ensure that the group's purpose is fulfilled. If it is not, the result is frustration, disharmony, criticism and, eventually perhaps, disintegration of the group.
3. *Maintain effective relationships* – between themselves and the members of the group, and between the people within the group. These relationships are effective if they contribute to achieving the task. They can be divided into those concerned with the team and its morale and sense of common purpose, and those concerned with individuals and how they are motivated.

These roles can be described in a number of ways as discussed below.

The John Adair three-circle model

John Adair (1973), the leading British expert on leadership, explains that these demands are best expressed as three areas of need which leaders are there to satisfy. These are: 1) task needs –

Figure 2.1   Leadership model: John Adair

to get the job done, 2) individual needs – to harmonize the needs of the individual with the needs of the task and the group and 3) group maintenance needs – to build and maintain team spirit. As shown in Figure 2.1, he models these demands as three interlocking circles.

This model suggests that the task, individual and group needs are interdependent. Satisfying task needs will also satisfy group and individual needs. Task needs, however, cannot be satisfied unless attention is paid to individual and group needs, and looking after individual needs will also contribute to satisfying group needs and vice versa. There is a danger in becoming so task orientated that you ignore individual and group or team needs. It is just as dangerous to be too people orientated, focusing on meeting individual or group needs at the expense of the task. The best leaders are those who keep these three needs satisfied and in balance according to the demands of the situation.

The path-goal model

The path-goal model states that leaders are there to define the path that should be followed by their team in order to achieve its goals. It is the leader's job to guide and help team members to select the best paths towards achieving their own goals and those of the group.

The Welch way

Jack Welch (2007), former chief executive of General Electric, has his own prescription for leadership. He writes:

> Being a leader changes everything. Before you are a leader success is all about you – your performance, contributions and solutions. Once you become a leader, success is all about growing others. It's about making the people who work for you smarter, bigger and bolder. Nothing you do as an individual matters, except how you nurture and support your team and increase their self-confidence. Your success as a leader will come not from what you do, but from the reflected glory of your team.

This is in line with the belief expressed by Charles Handy that the post-heroic leader has come to the fore who 'asks how every problem can be solved in a way that develops other people's capacity to handle it'. The Welch way also draws attention to the well-known phenomenon of people who are excellent at their non-managerial job but fail when they are promoted, for example successful sales representatives who become unsuccessful sales managers.

Leadership styles

There are many styles of leadership and no one style is necessarily better than the other in any situation. Leaders can be classified as:

- *Charismatic/non-charismatic.* **Charismatic leaders rely on their personality, their inspirational qualities and their 'aura'. They are visionary leaders who are achievement** orientated, calculated risk takers and good communicators. Non-charismatic leaders rely mainly on their know-how (authority goes to the person who knows), their quiet confidence and their cool, analytical approach to dealing with problems.

- *Autocratic/democratic.* Autocratic leaders impose their decisions, using their position to force people to do as they are told. Democratic leaders encourage people to participate and involve themselves in decision taking.
- *Enabler/controller.* Enablers inspire people with their vision of the future and empower them to accomplish team goals. Controllers command people to obtain their compliance.
- *Transactional/transformational.* Transactional leaders trade money, jobs and security for compliance. Transformational leaders motivate people to strive for higher level goals.

Another way of describing leadership styles is linked to the path-goal model. There are four styles:

1. *Achievement-orientated leadership* – the leader sets challenging goals for followers, expects them to perform at their highest level, and shows confidence in their ability to meet this expectation.
2. *Directive leadership* – the leader lets followers know what is expected of them and tells them how to perform their tasks.
3. *Participative leadership* – the leader consults with followers and asks for their suggestions before making a decision.
4. *Supportive leadership* – the leader is friendly and approachable and shows concern for the followers' well being.

But there is no such thing as an ideal leadership style. The situation in which leaders and their teams function will influence the approaches that leaders adopt. It all depends. The factors affecting the degree to which a style is appropriate will be the type of organization, the nature of the task, the characteristics of the group and, importantly, the personality of the leader.

An achievement-orientated approach may be appropriate when expectations of the results the team has to produce are high and team members can be encouraged to rise to the occasion.

A task-orientated approach (autocratic, controlling, directive) may be best in emergency or crisis situations or when the leader has power, formal backing and a relatively well-structured task. In these circumstances the group is more ready to be directed and told what to do. In less well-structured or ambiguous situations, where results depend on the group working well together with a common sense of purpose, leaders who are concerned with maintaining good relationships (democratic, participative or supportive) are more likely to obtain good results.

Good leaders are capable of flexing their style to meet the demands of the situation. Normally democratic or participative leaders may have to shift into more of a directive mode when faced with a crisis, but they make clear what they are doing and why. Poor leaders change their style arbitrarily so that their team members are confused and do not know what to expect next.

Effective leaders may also flex their style when dealing with individual team members according to their characteristics. Some people need more positive directions than others. Others respond best if they are involved in decision making with their boss. But there is a limit to the degree of flexibility that should be used. It is unwise to differentiate too much between the ways in which individuals are treated.

The kind of leadership exercised will indeed be related to the nature of the task and the people being led. But it also depends on the context and, of course, on leaders themselves. If you have a natural leadership style and it works, you have to be careful about changing it arbitrarily or substantially: modification yes, to a degree, transformation, no. And you can learn how to improve it as discussed towards the end of this chapter so that it fits the demands of the situation.

What makes a good leader?

What makes a good leader? There is no universal answer to this question. But Loo-Tzu in the 6th century BC had a pretty good stab at it:

> A leader is best
> When people barely know that he exists.
> Not so good when people obey and acclaim him.
> Worst when they despise him.
> Fail to honour people, they fail to honour you.
> But a good leader who talks little,
> When his work is done, his aim fulfilled,
> They will all say, 'We did this ourselves'.

More recent thinking about leadership has indicated that good leaders are confident and know where they want to go and what they want to do. They have the ability to take charge, convey their vision to their team, get their team members into action and ensure that they achieve their agreed goals. They are trustworthy, effective at influencing people and earn the respect of their team. They are aware of their own strengths and weaknesses and are skilled at understanding the needs, attitudes and perspective of team members. They appreciate the advantages of consulting and involving people in decision making. They can switch flexibly from one leadership style to another to meet the demands of different situations and people.

Many other lists and explanations of the qualities required by leaders have been produced, which complement or enhance the definition of a good leader given above. Here are a few of the better known ones.

John Adair

John Adair (1973) lists the following qualities good leaders possess:

- *enthusiasm* – to get things done, which they can communicate to other people;
- *confidence* – belief in themselves, which again people can sense (but this must not be over-confidence, which leads to arrogance);
- *toughness* – resilient, tenacious and demanding high standards, seeking respect but not necessarily popularity;
- *integrity* – being true to oneself – personal wholeness, soundness and honesty which inspires trust;
- *warmth* – in personal relationships, caring for people and being considerate;
- *humility* – willingness to listen and take the blame; not being arrogant and overbearing.

Leadership competencies

It was argued by Bennis and Thomas (2002) that the competencies of leaders (ie their skills, attributes and behaviours) are outcomes of their formative experiences. The key competencies are adaptive capacity, an ability to engage others in shared meanings, a compelling voice and integrity. They claim that one of the most reliable indicators and predictors of 'true leadership' is an individual's ability to find meaning in negative situations and to learn from trying circumstances.

The Industrial Society

An extensive survey conducted by the Industrial Survey (1997), now the Work Foundation, revealed that what good leaders do is to make the right space for people to perform well without having to be watched over. The top 10 requirements for leader behaviour as ranked by respondents were:

Rank	Factor
1	Shows enthusiasm
2	Supports other people
3	Recognizes individual effort
4	Listens to individuals' ideas and problems
5	Provides direction
6	Demonstrates personal integrity
7	Practises what he/she preaches
8	Encourages teamwork
9	Actively encourages feedback
10	Develops other people.

Leadership and emotional intelligence

Emotional intelligence has been defined by Goleman (2001) as 'the capacity for recognizing our own feelings and that of others, for motivating ourselves, for managing emotions well in ourselves as well as others'. He went on to say that 'you act with emotional intelligence when you are aware of and regulate your own emotions and when you are sensitive to what others are feeling and handle relationships accordingly'. An emotionally intelligent person understands his or her strengths and weaknesses and knows that it is more productive to manage emotions rather than be led by them.

Emotional intelligence, according to Goleman, is a critical ingredient in leadership. His research showed that effective leaders are alike in one crucial way: they have a high degree of emotional intelligence which plays an increasingly important part at higher levels in organizations where differences in technical skills are of negligible importance.

The components of emotional intelligence identified by Goleman are:

1. *Self-awareness* – the ability to recognize and understand your moods, emotions and drives as well as their effect on others. This is linked to three competencies: self-confidence, realistic self-assessment and a self-deprecating sense of humour.
2. *Self-regulation* – the ability to control or redirect disruptive impulses and moods and regulate own behaviour coupled with a propensity to pursue goals with energy and persistence. The three competencies associated with this component are trustworthiness and integrity, comfort with ambiguity, and openness to change.
3. *Motivation* – a passion to work for reasons that go beyond money and status and a propensity to pursue goals with energy and persistence. The three associated competencies are: strong drive to achieve, optimism, even in the face of failure, and organizational commitment.
4. *Empathy* – the ability to understand the emotional makeup of other people and skill in treating people according to their emotional reactions. This is linked to three competencies: expertise in building and retaining talent, cross-cultural sensitivity, and service to clients and customers.
5. *Social skills* – proficiency in managing relationships and building networks to get the desired result from others and reach personal goals and the ability to find common ground and build rapport. The three competencies associated with this component are: effectiveness in leading change, persuasiveness, and expertise in building and leading teams.

Leaders and followers

It is proposed by Robert Kelley (1991) that the role of the follower should be studied as carefully as that of the leader. Leaders need effective followers and one of the tasks of leaders is to develop what Kelley calls 'followship' qualities. These include the ability to manage themselves well, to be committed to the organization, to build their competence and focus their efforts for maximum impact.

A report on Robert Graves by his CO in the First World War said that 'The men will follow this young officer if only to know where he is going.' This is a good start but it is not enough. Followers want to feel that they are being led in the right direction. They need to know where they stand, where they are going and what is in it for them. They want to feel that it is all worth while. They have three requirements of their leaders:

1. *Leaders must fit their followers' expectations* – they are more likely to gain the respect and cooperation of their followers if they behave in ways that people expect from their leaders. These expectations will vary according to the group and the context but will often include being straight, fair and firm – as a 19th-century schoolboy once said of his headmaster: 'He's a beast but a just beast.' They also appreciate leaders who are considerate, friendly and approachable but don't want them to get too close – leaders who take too much time courting popularity are not liked.

2. *Leaders must be perceived as the 'best of us'* – they have to demonstrate that they are experts in the overall task facing the group. They need not necessarily have more expertise than any members of their group in particular aspects of the task, but they must demonstrate that they can get the group working purposefully together and direct and harness the expertise shared by group members to obtain results.

3. *Leaders must be perceived as 'the most of us'* – they must incorporate the norms and values which are central to the group. They can influence these values by visionary powers but they will fail if they move too far away from them.

Developing leadership skills

It is often said that leaders are born not made. This is a rather discouraging statement for those who are not leaders by birthright. It may be true to the extent that some people are visionaries, have built-in charisma and a natural ability to impose their personality on others. However, even they probably have to develop and hone these qualities when confronted with a situation demanding leadership. Ordinary mortals need not despair. They too can build on their natural capacities and develop their leadership abilities. A 10-point plan for doing this is given below.

A 10-point plan for developing leadership skills

1. Understand what is meant by leadership.
2. Appreciate the different leadership styles available.
3. Assess what you believe to be your fundamental leadership style.
4. Get other people, colleagues and indeed your own team members to tell you what they think your leadership style is and how well it works.
5. In the light of this information, consider what you need to do and can do to modify your style, bearing in mind that you have to go on being the same person. In other words, your style should still be a natural one.
6. Think about the typical situations and problems with which you are confronted as a leader. Will your leadership style, modified as necessary, be appropriate for all of them? If not, can you think of any of those situations where a different style

would have been better? If so, think about what you need to do to be able to flex your style as necessary without appearing to your team to be inconsistent.

7. Examine the various explanations of the qualities that make a good leader and assess your own performance using the checklist set out below. Decide what you need to do – what you can do – about any weaknesses.

8. Think about or observe any managers you know whom you have worked for or with.

9. Assess each of them in terms of the qualities using the checklist.

10. Consider what you can learn from them about effective and less effective leadership behaviours. In the light of this, assess where you could usefully modify your own leadership behaviours.

Assessing leadership skills

You can assess your own leadership skills or those of your boss by completing the questionnaire below. This could also be used by your team members to assess you – well worth while but it takes quite a lot of courage and determination to do it.

Leadership skills questionnaire

Please circle the number which most closely matches your opinion

Leadership behaviour	Strongly agree		Strongly disagree	
1 Makes clear to people what they have to do and achieve	4	3	2	1
2 Consistently gets good results	4	3	2	1
3 Encourages people to use their own initiative	4	3	2	1
4 Gives people sufficient scope to do their job	4	3	2	1
5 Gives people the guidance, coaching and support they need to do a good job	4	3	2	1
6 Gives regular feedback to people on their performance	4	3	2	1
7 Values the opinions of team members	4	3	2	1
8 Recognizes the achievements of the team and its individual members	4	3	2	1
9 Treats people fairly	4	3	2	1
10 Treats people with consideration	4	3	2	1

Leadership checklists

Task

- What needs to be done and why?
- What results have to be achieved and by when?
- What problems have to be overcome?
- To what extent are these problems straightforward?
- Is there a crisis situation?
- What has to be done now to deal with the crisis?
- What are these priorities?
- What pressures are likely to be exerted?

Individuals

- What are their strengths and weaknesses?
- What are likely to be the best ways of motivating them?
- What tasks are they best at doing?
- Is there scope to increase flexibility by developing new skills?
- How well do they perform in achieving targets and performance standards?
- To what extent can they manage their own performance and development?
- Are there any areas where there is a need to develop skill or competence?
- How can I provide them with the sort of support and guidance which will improve their performance?

Teams

- How well is the team organized?
- Does the team work well together?
- How can the commitment and motivation of the team be achieved?
- What is the team good and not so good at doing?

- What can I do to improve the performance of the team?
- Are team members flexible – capable of carrying out different tasks?
- To what extent can the team manage its own performance?
- Is there scope to empower the team so that it can take on greater responsibility for setting standards, monitoring performance and taking corrective action?
- Can the team be encouraged to work together to produce ideas for improving performance?

3

Motivating people

Leadership is about getting people into action and ensuring that they continue taking that action in order to achieve the task. It is therefore very much about motivation. This can be defined as the process of getting people to move in the direction you want them to go. The organization as a whole provides the context within which high levels of motivation can be achieved through reward systems and the provision of opportunities for growth and development. But as a manager you still have a major part to play in deploying your own motivating skills to ensure that people give of their best. You want them to exert the maximum amount of positive discretionary effort – people often have a choice about how they carry out their work and the amount of care, innovation and productive behaviour they display. Discretionary effort makes the difference between people just doing a job and people doing a great job.

You have to remember that while the organization may have motivational processes in place such as performance-related pay, you cannot rely upon them alone. You are the person in day-to-day contact with employees and in the last analysis their motivation depends on you.

Unfortunately, approaches to motivation are too often underpinned by simplistic assumptions about how it works. The process of motivation is much more complex than many people believe and motivational practices are most likely to function effectively if they are based on proper understanding of what is involved.

This chapter therefore:

- **defines motivation;**
- **offers a somewhat simplified explanation of the basic process of motivation;**
- **describes the two basic types of motivation – intrinsic and extrinsic;**
- **explores in greater depth the various theories of motivation which explain and amplify the basic process;**
- **examines the practical implications of the motivation theories.**

The final section of the chapter deals with the associated concept of engagement which has come to the fore, at least in human resource management circles, in recent years.

What follows is based on the huge amount of practical research that has provided the basis for the development of motivation theory. But don't let the word 'theory' put you off. It has been said that 'there is nothing so practical as a good theory', by which is meant that theories based on extensive research in the field, ie within organizations, can reveal what approaches work best and how to put them into practice. A good example is that of two American researchers, Gary Latham and Edwin Locke, who developed their goal-setting theory of motivation by studying 1,184 supervisors and finding that those who set specific production goals achieved the highest productivity. Their further analysis of 10 field studies conducted by various researchers for a range of jobs showed that the percentage change in performance after goal setting ranged from 11 to 27 per cent (average 16 per cent).

Motivation defined

A motive is a reason for doing something. Motivation is concerned with the factors that influence people to behave in certain ways. Motivating other people is about getting them to move in the direction you want them to go in order to achieve a result.

The three components of motivation are:

- **direction – what a person is trying to do;**
- **effort – how hard a person is trying;**
- **persistence – how long a person keeps on trying.**

Motivation can be described as goal-directed behaviour. Well-motivated people are those with clearly defined goals who take action which they expect will achieve those goals. Such people may be self-motivated, and, as long as this means they are going in the right direction to achieve what they are there to achieve, this is the best form of motivation. Most of us, however, need to be motivated to a greater or lesser degree.

The process of motivation

Motivation is initiated by the conscious or unconscious recognition of an unsatisfied need. A goal is then established which it is believed will satisfy this need and a decision is made on the action which it is expected will achieve the goal. If the goal is achieved the need will be satisfied and the behaviour is likely to be repeated the next time a similar need emerges. If the goal is not achieved the same action is less likely to be repeated. This process is modelled in Figure 3.1.

From an organizational point of view, the model can be used to illustrate a process of motivation which involves setting goals that are likely to meet individual needs and encouraging the behaviour required to achieve those goals. It also illustrates two

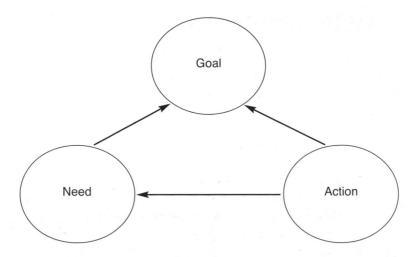

Figure 3.1   The process of motivation

fundamental truths about motivation. First, that there is a multiplicity of needs, goals and actions which depend on the person and the situation. It is unwise to assume that any one approach to motivation will appeal to all affected by it. Motivation policies and practices must recognize that people are different. Second, that while we can observe how people behave – the actions they take – we cannot be certain about what has motivated them to behave that way, ie what are the needs and goals that have affected their actions.

How motivation takes place

There are two types of motivation:

1. *Intrinsic motivation* – the aspects of the work they do and the work environment which create job satisfaction and influence people to behave in a particular way or to move

in a particular direction. These factors include responsibility (feeling that the work is important and having control over one's own resources), freedom to act (autonomy), scope to use and develop skills and abilities, interesting and challenging work and opportunities for advancement.

2. *Extrinsic motivation* – what is done to or for people to motivate them. This includes rewards, such as increased pay, praise or promotion, and punishments, such as disciplinary action, withholding pay, or criticism.

Extrinsic motivators can have an immediate and powerful effect, but it will not necessarily last long. The intrinsic motivators, which are concerned with the 'quality of working life' (a phrase and movement which emerged from this concept), are likely to have a deeper and longer term effect because they are inherent in the work and the work environment and are not imposed from outside. However, managers can exert considerable influence on the work environment and this can be a powerful motivational tool.

Motivation theories

The process of motivation as described above is broadly based on a number of motivation theories which attempt to explain in more detail what it is all about. These theories have proliferated over the years. Some of them, like the crude 'instrumentality' theory which was the first to be developed and is essentially a 'carrot and stick' approach to motivation, have largely been discredited, at least in psychological circles, although they still underpin the beliefs of some managers about motivation and pay systems. Others such as those developed by Maslow and Herzberg are no longer highly regarded because they are not supported by field research (Maslow) or because the field research was flawed (Herzberg). However, Maslow did contribute the useful notions

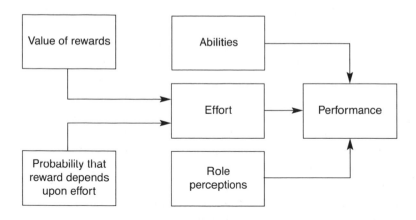

Figure 3.2 Motivation expectancy theory model (Porter and Lawler, 1968)

The key messages of motivation theory

The key messages provided by motivation theory are summarized below.

Extrinsic and intrinsic motivating factors

Extrinsic rewards provided by the employer, including pay, will be important in attracting and retaining employees and, for limited periods, increasing effort and minimizing dissatisfaction. Intrinsic rewards related to responsibility, achievement and the work itself may have a longer term and deeper impact on motivation.

The significance of needs and wants

People will be better motivated if their work experience satisfies their social and psychological needs as well as their economic needs.

The influence of goals

Individuals at work are motivated by having specific goals, and they perform better when they are aiming for difficult goals which they have accepted and when they receive feedback on performance.

The importance of expectations

The degree to which people are motivated will depend not only upon the perceived value of the outcome of their actions – the goal or reward – but also upon their perceptions of the likelihood of obtaining a worthwhile reward, ie their expectations. They will be highly motivated if they can control the means to attain their goals.

Approaches to motivation

Taking the lessons learnt from motivation theory into account, the approaches you can adopt to motivating people can be classified under three headings:

1. valuing people;
2. rewarding them financially;
3. providing non-financial rewards.

Valuing people

Motivation will be enhanced if people feel that they are valued. This means investing in their success, trusting and empowering them, giving them the opportunity to be involved in matters with which they are concerned, keeping them fully in the picture, treating them fairly and like human beings, rather than 'resources' to be exploited in the interests of management, and providing them with rewards (financial and non-financial) which demonstrate the extent to which they are valued.

Financial rewards

Money, in the form of pay or some other sort of remuneration, is the most obvious form of reward. Money provides the carrot which most people want.

However, doubts have been cast on the effectiveness of money as a motivator by Herzberg et al (1957) because, they claimed, while the lack of it can cause dissatisfaction, its provision does not result in lasting satisfaction. There is something in this, especially for people on fixed salaries or rates of pay who do not benefit directly from an incentive scheme. They may feel good when they get an increase; apart from the extra money, it is a highly tangible form of recognition and an effective means of helping people to feel that they are valued. But this feeling of euphoria can rapidly die away. Other dissatisfactions from Herzberg's list of hygiene factors, such as working conditions or the quality of management, can loom larger in some people's minds when they fail to get the satisfaction they need from the work itself. However, it must be re-emphasized that different people have different needs and wants; some will be much more motivated by money than others. What cannot be assumed is that money motivates everyone in the same way and to the same extent. Thus it is naive to think that the introduction of a performance-related scheme will miraculously transform everyone overnight into well-motivated, high-performing individuals.

Nevertheless, money provides the means to achieve a number of different ends. It is a powerful force because it is linked directly or indirectly to the satisfaction of many needs. It clearly satisfies basic needs for survival and security, if it is coming in regularly. It can also satisfy the need for self-esteem (it is a visible mark of appreciation) and status – money can set you in a grade apart from your fellows and can buy you things they can't to build up your prestige. Money satisfies the less desirable but still prevalent drives of acquisitiveness and cupidity.

Money may in itself have no intrinsic meaning, but it acquires significant motivating power because it comes to symbolize so many intangible goals. It acts as a symbol in different ways for different people, and for the same person at different times. And pay is often the dominant factor in the choice of employer and pay considerations are powerful in binding people to their present job.

But do financial incentives motivate people? The answer is yes, for those people who are strongly motivated by money and whose expectations that they will receive a financial reward are high. But less confident employees may not respond to incentives which they do not expect to achieve. It can also be argued that extrinsic rewards may erode intrinsic interest – people who work just for money could find their tasks less pleasurable and may not, therefore, do them so well. What we do know is that a multiplicity of factors is involved in performance improvements and many of those factors are interdependent.

Money can therefore provide positive motivation in the right circumstances not only because people need and want money but also because it serves as a highly tangible means of recognition. But badly designed and managed pay systems can demotivate. Another researcher in this area was Eliot Jaques (1961), who emphasized the need for such systems to be perceived as being fair and equitable. In other words, the reward should be clearly related to effort or level of responsibility and people should not receive less money than they deserve compared with their fellow workers. Jaques called this the 'felt fair' principle.

Non-financial rewards

From your point of view as a people manager, money is not only an unreliable motivator but its provision as an incentive is often outside your control. Many public sector organizations and many charities have pay spines in which pay progression is dependent on service rather than performance and line managers have little or no impact on the rate at which they progress. Even when pay is related to performance, line managers have to live with the system adopted by the organization. Their influence is often limited to rating people's performance but the amount distributed is probably controlled by the management. But they can have much more control over non-financial rewards, including the intrinsic rewards which, as noted above, can have a powerful and long-lasting effect on motivation. The main non-financial rewards as discussed below are recognition, achievement, responsibility and autonomy, and opportunities for personal development and growth.

Recognition

Recognition is one of the most effective methods of motivating people. They need to know not only how well they have achieved their objectives or carried out their work but also that their achievements are appreciated.

Recognition can be provided by positive and immediate feedback from you which acknowledges what has been achieved. Simply saying thank you and explaining why may be enough. You also recognize people when you listen to and act upon their suggestions. Other actions which provide recognition include allocation to a high-profile project, enlargement of the job to provide scope for more interesting and rewarding work and recommending promotion or inclusion in a high-profile development programme.

Public 'applause' – letting everyone know that someone has done well – is another form of recognition. But it must be used with care. One person's recognition implies an element of non-recognition to others and the consequences of having winners and losers need to be carefully managed.

Many organizations have formal recognition schemes which give managers scope, including a budget, to provide individuals (and importantly, through them, their partners) with tangible means of recognition in the forms of gifts, vouchers, holidays or trips in the UK or abroad, days or weekends at health spas, or meals out. Team awards may be through outings, parties and meals. Managers can provide individuals and teams with small recognition rewards from their budget and can nominate people for larger awards.

The principles you need to bear in mind in providing recognition are that it:

- **should be given for specially valued behaviours and exceptional effort as well as for special achievements;**
- **is about valuing people; it should be personalized so that people appreciate that it applies to them;**
- **needs to be applied equitably, fairly and consistently throughout your team;**
- **must be genuine, not used as a mechanistic motivating device;**
- **needs to be given as soon as possible after the achievement;**
- **should be available to all;**
- **should be available for teams as well as individuals to reward collective effort and avoid creating isolated winners.**

Achievement

People feel rewarded and motivated if they have the scope to achieve as well as being recognized for the achievement. University researchers, for example, want to enhance their reputation as well as making a significant contribution to their institution's research rating.

If achievement motivation is high it will result in

discretionary behaviour. Discretionary or self-motivated behaviour occurs when people take control of situations or relationships, direct the course of events, create and seize opportunities, enjoy challenge, react swiftly and positively to new circumstances and relationships, and generally 'make things happen'. People who are driven by the need to achieve are likely to be proactive, to seek opportunities and to insist on recognition. You can develop achievement motivation by ensuring people know what they are expected to achieve, giving them the opportunity to achieve, providing the support and guidance that will enable them to achieve and recognizing their achievements.

Responsibility and autonomy

You can motivate people by giving them more responsibility for their own work and more autonomy in the sense that they can make their own decisions without reference to you. This is in line with the concept of intrinsic motivation which emphasizes that a major influence on motivation is provided by the work itself – people are motivated when they are provided with the means to achieve their goals. The scope for designing or redesigning roles varies according to the nature of the work. But where there is an opportunity it is worth seizing, and methods of doing so are examined in the next chapter.

Opportunity to develop

Most people want to develop – to get a better or more interesting job and to advance their careers either through promotion or laterally by expanding their roles. You can use this need as a motivator by providing learning and development opportunities, making use of what is available in the organization but also giving people additional responsibilities so that they gain experience with whatever support and guidance you need to give them.

10 steps to achieving higher motivation

1. Agree demanding but achievable goals.
2. Create expectations that certain behaviours and outputs will produce worthwhile rewards when people succeed.
3. Provide feedback on performance.
4. Design jobs which enable people to feel a sense of accomplishment, to express and use their abilities and to exercise their own decision-making powers.
5. Make good use of the organization's reward system to provide appropriate financial incentives.
6. Provide recognition and praise for work well done.
7. Communicate to your team and its members the link between performance and reward, thus enhancing expectations.
8. Provide effective leadership.
9. Give people the guidance and training which will develop the knowledge and skills they need to improve their performance and be rewarded accordingly.
10. Offer opportunities for learning and development which will enable them to advance their careers.

Engagement

Engagement takes place when people are committed to their work. They are interested, indeed excited, about what they do. It can exist even when individuals are not committed to the organization except in so far as it gives them the opportunity and scope to perform and to develop their skills and potential. They may be more attached to the type of work they carry out than to

the organization that provides that work, especially if they are
knowledge workers. Getting job engagement is more likely when
people feel empowered, as discussed at the end of this chapter.

Developing job engagement

Developing job engagement starts with job design or 'role
development'. This will focus on the provision of:

- *interest and challenge* – **the degree to which the work is
  interesting in itself and creates demanding goals for
  people;**
- *variety* – **the extent to which the activities in the job call
  for a selection of skills and abilities;**
- *autonomy* – **the freedom and independence the job
  holder has, including discretion to make decisions,
  exercise choice, schedule the work and decide on the
  procedures to carry it out, and the job holder's personal
  responsibility for outcomes;**
- *task identity* – **the degree to which the job requires
  completion of a whole and identifiable piece of work;**
- *task significance* – **the extent to which the job
  contributes to a significant end result and has a
  substantial impact on the lives and work of other
  people.**

All these factors are affected by the quality of leadership. The
latter is vital. You can make a major contribution to achieving job
engagement and therefore higher performance by the way in
which you lead people, and this includes making an effort to
ensure that their jobs have the characteristics set out above. All
this depends more on the way in which you manage and lead job
holders than on any formal process of job design. You often have
considerable discretion on how you allocate work and the extent
to which you delegate. You can provide feedback which
recognizes the contribution of people and you can spell out the
significance of the work they do.

Empowering people

Job engagement is increased if people are empowered, ie they have more 'power' or scope to exercise control over and take responsibility for their work. It means allowing them more autonomy. Empowerment releases the creative and innovative capacities of people and provides for greater job satisfaction, motivation and commitment. It is about engaging both the hearts and minds of people so that they can take the opportunities available to them for increased responsibility. Ten ways of empowering people are set out below.

1. Delegate more.
2. Involve people in setting their targets and standards of performance and in deciding on performance measures.
3. Allow individuals and teams more scope to plan, act and monitor their own performance.
4. Involve people in developing their own solutions to problems.
5. Create self-managed teams – ones that set their own objectives and standards and manage their own performance.
6. Give people a voice in deciding what needs to be done.
7. Help people to learn from their own mistakes.
8. Encourage continuous development so that people can both grow in their roles and grow their roles.
9. Share your vision and plans with members of your team.
10. Trust people and treat them as adults.

4

Organizing

The management of people in organizations constantly raises questions such as 'Who does what?', 'How should activities be grouped together?', 'What lines and means of communication need to be established?', 'How should people be helped to understand their roles in relation to the objectives of their team and the organization and the roles of their colleagues?' and 'Are we doing everything that we ought to be doing and nothing that we ought not to be doing?'

As a manager or team leader you might have been promoted, transferred or recruited into your post and have been presented with an established organization structure – a framework for getting things done. Very occasionally, you may have to set up your own organization. More frequently, you may feel that there are improvements which can usefully be made to the structure or to the ways in which responsibilities and tasks are allocated to members of your team. To do this it is useful to understand the process and aim of organizing, the guidelines available on organizing, the approach to job design and how to define roles, as explained in this chapter.

The process of organizing

The process of organizing can be described as the design, development and maintenance of a system of coordinated activities in which individuals and groups of people work cooperatively under leadership towards commonly understood and accepted goals. This may involve the grand design or redesign of the total structure, but most frequently it is concerned with the organization of particular functions and activities and the basis upon which the relationships between them are managed.

There are two important points to bear in mind about organizations. First, organizations are not static things. Changes are constantly taking place in the business itself, in the environment in which the business operates, and in the people who work in the business. Second, organizations consist of people working more or less cooperatively together. Inevitably, and especially at managerial levels, the organization may have to be adjusted to fit the particular strengths and attributes of the people available. The result may not conform to the ideal, but it is more likely to work than a structure that ignores the human element. It is always desirable to have an ideal structure in mind, but it is equally desirable to modify it to meet particular circumstances, as long as there is awareness of the potential problems that may arise. This may seem an obvious point, but it is frequently ignored by management consultants and others who adopt a doctrinaire approach to organization, sometimes with disastrous results.

Aim

Bearing in mind the need to take an empirical approach to organizing, the aim of organizing could be defined as being to optimize the arrangements for conducting the affairs of the business or business unit. To do this it is necessary, as far as circumstances allow, to:

- clarify the overall purposes of the organization or organizational unit;
- define the key activities required to achieve that purpose;
- group these activities logically together to avoid unnecessary overlap or duplication;
- provide for the integration of activities and the achievement of cooperative effort and teamwork in pursuit of the common purpose;
- build flexibility into the system so that organizational arrangements can adapt quickly to new situations and challenges;
- clarify individual roles, accountabilities and authorities;
- design jobs to make the best use of the skills and capacities of the job holders and to provide them with high levels of intrinsic motivation.

Organizational guidelines

No absolute standards exist against which an organization structure can be judged. There is no such thing as an ideal organization; there is never one right way of organizing anything and there are no absolute principles which govern organizational choice. But there are some guidelines as described below which you can refer to if faced with the job of setting up or reviewing an organization. They are not absolutes but they are worth considering in the light of your analysis of the needs of the situation:

- *Allocation of work* – the work that has to be done should be defined and allocated to work teams, project groups and individual positions. Related activities should be grouped together.

- *Differentiation and integration* – it is necessary to differentiate between the different activities that have to be carried out, but it is equally necessary to ensure that these activities are integrated so that everyone in the team is working towards the same goals.
- *Teamwork* – jobs should be defined and roles described in ways that facilitate and underline the importance of teamwork. Areas where cooperation is required should be emphasized. Wherever possible, self-managing teams should be set up with the maximum amount of responsibility to run their own affairs, including planning, budgeting and exercising quality control. Networking should be encouraged in the sense of people communicating openly and informally with one another as the need arises. It should be recognized that these informal processes can be more productive than rigidly 'working through channels' as set out in an organization chart.
- *Flexibility* – the structure should be flexible enough to respond quickly to change, challenge and uncertainty. At management levels a 'collegiate' approach to team operation should be considered in which people share responsibility and are expected to work with their colleagues in areas outside their primary function or skill.
- *Role clarification* – people should be clear about their roles as individuals and as members of a team. They should know what they will be held accountable for and be given every opportunity to use their abilities in achieving objectives which they have agreed and are committed to. Role profiles should define key result areas but should not act as straitjackets, restricting initiative and unduly limiting responsibility. Elaborate job descriptions listing every task are unnecessary as they limit flexibility and authority and, because they appear to be comprehensive, invite some people to make the remark that 'It is not in my job description.'

- *Decentralization* – authority to make decisions should be delegated as close to the scene of action as possible.
- *Delayering* – too many layers create unnecessary 'pecking orders', inhibit communications and limit flexibility.
- *Span of control* – there is a limit to the number of people one manager or team leader can control, although this limit varies according to the nature of the work and the people who carry it out. In fact, you can work with a far larger span than you imagine as long as you are prepared to delegate more, to avoid becoming involved in too much detail and concentrate on developing good teamwork.
- *'One-over-one' relationships* – situations in which a single manager controls another single manager who in turn controls a team of people can cause confusion as to who is in charge and how the duties of the two people in the one-over-one relationship are divided.
- *One person one boss* – ideally individuals should be responsible to one person so that they know where they stand. One of the main exceptions to this rule occurs when someone has a direct 'line' responsibility to a manager but also has a 'functional' responsibility to a senior member of the individual's function, who is concerned with maintaining corporate standards for the function and dealing with corporate policies. But in such cases the way in which functional responsibility is exercised and its limits have to be defined and, usually, it is understood that individuals are accountable to their line manager for achieving results within their department or team.

Job design

Unless you are responsible for entirely prescribed production-line-type operations there is likely to be some scope for you to influence the way in which the jobs in your unit are designed. Job design involves deciding on the content of jobs, that is, the responsibilities, duties or tasks that should be grouped together in a single job. This means analysing the overall task which the team exists to achieve in order to establish the activities that need to be carried out, and dividing these activities between the members of the team.

Job design has three aims: first, to ensure that the work that needs to be done gets done; second, to provide the maximum degree of intrinsic motivation and job engagement for those who have to carry out the work; and third, to fulfil the social responsibilities of the organization to the people who work in it by improving the quality of their working life.

There are 10 steps you can take to ensure that these aims are achieved.

1. Where possible, arrange for people to work on a complete activity or product, or a significant part of it which can be seen as a whole.
2. Combine interdependent tasks into a job.
3. Provide a variety of tasks within the job.
4. Arrange work in a way that allows individuals to influence their work methods and pace.
5. Include tasks that offer some degree of autonomy for employees in the sense of making their own decisions.
6. Ensure that individuals can receive feedback about how well they are doing, preferably by evaluating their performance themselves.
7. Provide employees with the information they need to monitor their performance and make decisions.
8. Provide internal and external customer feedback directly to employees.

9. As far as possible, ensure that the job is perceived by individuals as requiring them to use abilities they value in order to perform it effectively.
10. Provide opportunities for employees to achieve outcomes that they consider desirable such as personal advancement in the form of increased pay, scope for developing expertise, improved status within a work group and a more challenging job.

Developing role profiles

As part of the process of organizing work you need to ensure that everyone is aware of what they have to achieve, the knowledge and skills they need and how they are expected to carry out their job. This means developing role profiles in conjunction with job holders. It is essential that they take part in this process to maximize the degree to which they understand and accept their role requirements. A role profile is much more than the list of tasks included in a conventional job description. As the name implies, role profiles emphasize more strongly the parts that people are expected to play in terms of the outcomes they are expected to achieve and how they are expected to behave (behavioural competencies) in, for example, upholding organizational values. Role profiles also spell out what role holders need to know and be able to do – their knowledge and skills requirements.

To develop a role profile it is necessary for you to get together with the individual members of your team to agree the key result areas, knowledge and skills and behavioural competencies they need. The sort of questions you can ask to obtain this information include:

- **What do you think are the most important things you have to do?**

- What do you believe you are expected to achieve in each of these areas?
- How will you – or anyone else – know whether or not you have achieved them?
- What have you to know and be able to do to perform effectively in these areas?
- What knowledge and skills in terms of qualifications, technical and procedural knowledge, problem-solving, planning and communication skills etc do you need to carry out the role effectively?
- How do you think someone in this role should behave in getting the work done? (Reference can be made to a published set of core values or a competency framework defining key behaviours if these are available.)

If you have an HR (human resources) department, you should be able to obtain advice and help in preparing profiles.

Role profile definition

Role profiles can be set out under the following headings:

- *Role title*
- *Department*
- *Responsible to*
- *Responsible to role holder*
- *Purpose of the role* – defined in one reasonably succinct sentence which defines why the role exists in terms of the overall contribution the role holder makes.
- *Key result areas* – if at all possible these should be limited to seven or eight, certainly not more than ten. Each key result area should be defined in a single sentence which describes the purpose of the activity in terms of the outcomes to be achieved.
- *Need to know* – the knowledge required overall or in specific key result areas of the business and its

competitors and customers, techniques, processes, procedures or products.

- *Need to be able to do* – the skills required in each area of activity.
- *Expected behaviour* – the behaviours particularly expected of the role holder (behavioural competencies), which may be extracted from the organization's competency framework or statement of core values.

An example of a role profile is given in Figure 4.1.

Role title: Database administrator

Department: Information systems

Purpose of role: Responsible for the development and support of databases and their underlying environment.

Key result areas
- Identify database requirements for all projects that require data management in order to meet the needs of internal customers.
- Develop project plans collaboratively with colleagues to deliver against their database needs.
- Support underlying database infrastructure.
- Liaise with system and software providers to obtain product information and support.
- Manage project resources (people and equipment) within predefined budget and criteria, as agree with line manager and originating department.
- Allocate work to and supervise contractors on day-to-day basis.
- Ensure security of the underlying database infrastructure through adherence to established protocols and to develop additional security protocols where needed.

Need to know
- Oracle database administration.
- Operation of Oracle RDBMS, SQL*Plus and BPEL Process Manager.

Able to:
- Analyse and choose between options where the solution is not always obvious.
- Develop project plans and organize own workload on a timescale of 1–2 months.
- Adapt to rapidly changing needs and priorities without losing sight of overall plans and priorities.
- Interpret budgets in order to manage resources effectively within them.

- Negotiate with suppliers.
- Keep abreast of technical developments and trends, bring these into day-to-day work when feasible and build them into new project developments.

Behavioural competencies
- Aim to get things done well and set and meet challenging goals.
- Analyse information from a range of sources and develop effective solutions/recommendations.
- Communicate clearly and persuasively, orally or in writing, dealing with technical issues in a non-technical manner.
- Work participatively on projects with technical and non-technical colleagues.
- Develop positive relationships with colleagues as the supplier of an internal service.

Figure 4.1   Example of a role profile

5

Team building

One of your most important roles as a manager is to act as a team builder – developing and making the best use of the capacity of your team so that its members jointly deliver superior levels of performance.

Team building takes place when you clarify the team's purpose and goals, ensure that its members work well together, strengthen the team's collective skills, enhance commitment and confidence, remove externally imposed obstacles and create opportunities for team members to develop their skills and competencies.

To undertake this task you need to get answers to these questions:

- **What is a team?**
- **What are the characteristics of teams?**
- **What are the factors that contribute to team effectiveness?**
- **How should team performance be assessed?**
- **How should team performance reviews be conducted?**
- **And overall, what needs to be done to obtain good teamwork?**

What is a team?

A team is a group of people with complementary skills who work together to achieve a common purpose. Their team leader sets the direction, provides guidance and support, coordinates the team's activities, ensures that each team member plays his or her part, promotes the learning and development of team members, consults with the team on issues affecting its work and, in conjunction with team members, monitors and reviews team performance.

However, some organizations have developed the concept of self-managing teams which are largely autonomous, responsible to a considerable degree for planning and scheduling work, problem solving, developing their own key performance indicators and setting and monitoring team performance and quality standards. The role of their team leaders is primarily to act as coordinators and facilitators; their style is expected to be more supportive and facilitative than directive.

What are the characteristics of teams?

In their influential book *The Magic of Teams*, Katzenbach and Smith (1993) suggested that the characteristics of teams were as follows:

- **Teams are the basic units of performance for most organizations. They meld together the skills, experiences and insights of several people.**
- **Teamwork applies to the whole organization as well as to specific teams. It represents a set of values that encourage behaviours such as listening and responding cooperatively to points of view expressed by others, giving others the benefit of the doubt, providing support to those who need it and recognizing the interests and achievements of others.**

- Teams are created and energized by significant and demanding performance challenges.
- Teams outperform individuals acting alone or in large organizational groupings, especially when performance requires multiple skills, judgements and experiences.
- Teams are flexible and responsive to changing events and demands. They can adjust their approach to new information and challenges with greater speed, accuracy and effectiveness than can individuals caught in the web of larger organizational connections.
- Successful teams invest much time and effort exploring, shaping and agreeing on a purpose that belongs to them, both collectively and individually. They are characterized by a deep sense of commitment to achieving high levels of performance.

What are the factors that contribute to team effectiveness?

An effective team is likely to be one in which its purpose is clear and its members feel the task is important, both to them and to the organization. The structure, leadership and methods of operation are relevant to the requirements of the task. Team members will be highly engaged in the work they do together and committed to the whole group task. They will have been grouped together in a way that means they are related to one another through the requirements of task performance and task interdependence. The team will use discretionary effort – going the extra mile – to ensure that its work gets done.

The following is a selection of some of the key competencies for team members as developed by Hay/McBer:

- *interpersonal understanding* – accurate interpretation of others' concerns, motives and feelings and recognition of their strengths and weaknesses;

- *influence* – using appropriate interpersonal styles and logical arguments to convince others to accept ideas or pleas;
- *customer service orientation* – demonstrating concern for meeting the needs of internal and external customers;
- *adaptability* – adapting easily to change;
- teamwork and cooperation – developing collaborative work which generates acceptable solutions;
- *oral communication* – expressing ideas in group situations;
- achievement orientation – setting and meeting challenging objectives;
- *organizational commitment* – performing work with broader organizational goals in mind.

The main features of well-functioning teams as described by Douglas McGregor (1960) are that the atmosphere tends to be informal, comfortable and relaxed; team members listen to each other; most decisions are reached by consensus; when action is taken, clear assignments are made and accepted, and team leaders do not dominate their teams – the issue is not who controls but how to get the work done.

How should team performance be assessed?

The performance of teams should be assessed in terms of their output and results and the quality of team processes that have contributed to those results.

Output criteria include the achievement of team goals, customer satisfaction and the quantity and quality of work. Process measures comprise participation, collaboration and collective effort, conflict resolution, joint decision making, planning and goal setting, interpersonal relations, interdependence and adaptability and flexibility.

How you and your team apply these criteria will be related to the following factors that affect team performance:

- **the clarity of the team's goals in terms of expectations and priorities;**
- **how work is allocated to the team;**
- **how the team is working (its processes) in terms of cohesion, ability to handle internal conflict and pressure, relationships with other teams;**
- **the extent to which the team is capable of managing itself – setting goals and priorities, monitoring performance;**
- **the quality of leadership – even self-managed teams need a sense of direction which they cannot necessarily generate by themselves;**
- **the level and range of skills possessed by individual team members;**
- **the extent to which team members work flexibly, taking advantage of the multi-skilling capabilities of its members;**
- **the systems and resources support available to the team.**

How should team performance reviews be conducted?

Good support to your team-building efforts will be provided if you conduct regular team performance review meetings to assess feedback and control information on their joint achievements against objectives and to discuss any issues concerning team work. The agenda for such meetings could be as follows:

1. General feedback review of the progress of the team as a whole, problems encountered by the team which have caused difficulties or hampered progress, and helps and hindrances to the operation of the team.

2. Work reviews of how well the team has functioned.
3. Group problem solving, including an analysis of reasons for any shortfalls or other problems and agreement of what needs to be done to solve them and prevent their re-occurrence.
4. Update objectives – review of new requirements, opportunities or threats and the amendment of objectives as required.

Use can be made of the 10-point checklist given in the box.

Checklist for analysing team performance

1. How effective are we at achieving team goals?
2. How well do we work together?
3. Does everyone contribute?
4. How effectively is the team led?
5. How good are we at analysing problems and making decisions?
6. How good are we at initiating action?
7. Do we concentrate sufficiently on the priority issues?
8. Do we waste time on irrelevancies?
9. To what extent can team members speak their minds without being squashed by others?
10. If there is any conflict, is it openly expressed and is it about issues rather than personalities?

What needs to be done to achieve good teamwork?

The following are 10 things to do when building your team:

1. Establish urgency and direction.
2. Select members based on skills and skill potential who are good at working with others but still capable of taking their own line when necessary.
3. Pay particular attention to first meetings and actions.
4. Agree with team members immediate performance-orientated tasks and goals, including overlapping or interlocking objectives for people who work together. These will take the form of targets to be achieved or tasks to be accomplished by joint action.
5. Assess people's performance not only on the results they achieve but also on the degree to which they are good team members. Recognize people who have been good team workers.
6. Recognize good team performance by praise and rewards for the team as a whole.
7. Build team spirit by out-of-work activities.
8. Hold team meetings to review performance, focusing on team process as well as outputs.
9. Provide learning and development opportunities so that team members can become multi-skilled or at least improve the level of their existing skills.
10. Make use of any learning activities provided by the organization that focus on teamwork.

6

Delegating

You can't do everything yourself, so you have to delegate. It is one of the most important things you do. At first sight delegation looks simple. Just tell people what you want them to do and then let them get on with it. But there is more to it than that. It is not easy. It requires courage, patience and skill. And it is an aspect of your work in which you have more freedom of choice than in any other of your activities. What you choose to delegate, to whom and how, is almost entirely at your discretion.

This chapter provides answers to the following questions about delegation:

- **What is it?**
- **What are its advantages?**
- **What are the difficulties?**
- **When do you delegate?**
- **How do you delegate?**
- **How can you assess whether you are good at delegating?**

What is delegation?

Delegation is not the same as handing out work. There are some things that your team members do that go with the territory. They are part of their normal duties and all you have to do is to define what those duties are and allocate work accordingly.

Delegation is different. It takes place when you deliberately give someone the authority to carry out a piece of work which you could have decided to keep and carry out yourself. Bear in mind that what you are doing is delegating authority to carry out a task and make the decisions this involves. You are still accountable for the results achieved. It is sometimes said that you cannot delegate responsibility but this is misleading if responsibility is defined, as it usually is, as what people are expected to do – their work, their tasks and their duties. What you cannot do is delegate accountability. In the last analysis, you as the manager or team leader always carries the can. What managers have to do is to ensure that people have the authority to carry out their responsibilities. A traffic warden without the power to issue tickets would have to be exceedingly persuasive to have any chance of dealing with parking offences.

What are the advantages of delegation?

The advantages of delegation are that it:

- **enables you to focus on the things that really matter in your job – those aspects which require your personal experience, skill and knowledge;**
- **relieves you of less critical and routine tasks;**
- **frees you from being immersed in detail;**
- **extends your capacity to manage;**
- **reduces delay in decision making – as long as authority is delegated close to the scene of action;**

- allows decisions to be taken at the level where the details are known;
- empowers and motivates your staff by extending their responsibilities and authority and providing them with greater autonomy;
- develops the knowledge and skills of your staff and increases their capacity to exercise judgement and make decisions.

What are the difficulties of delegation?

The advantages of delegation are compelling but there are difficulties. The main problem is that delegation often involves risk. You cannot be absolutely sure that the person to whom you have delegated something will carry out the work as you would wish. The temptation therefore is to over-supervise, breathe down people's necks and interfere. This inhibits their authority, makes them nervous and resentful and destroys their confidence, thus dissipating any advantages the original act of delegation might have had. Another difficulty is that many managers are reluctant to delegate because they want to keep on top of everything. They really think they know best and cannot trust any one else to do it as well, never mind better. Finally, some managers are reluctant to delegate simply because they enjoy what they are doing and cannot bear the possibility of giving it away to anyone else.

Approaches to delegation

To a degree, overcoming these difficulties is a matter of simply being aware of them and appreciating that if there are any disadvantages, these are outweighed by the advantages. But

approaches to delegation such as those discussed below help.
You need to understand the process of delegation, when to
delegate, what to delegate, how to choose people to whom you
want to delegate, how to give out the work and how to monitor
performance.

The process of delegation

Delegation is a process which starts from the point when total
control is exercised (no freedom of action for the individual to
whom work has been allocated) to full devolution (the individual
is completely empowered to carry out the work). This sequence is
illustrated in Figure 6.1.

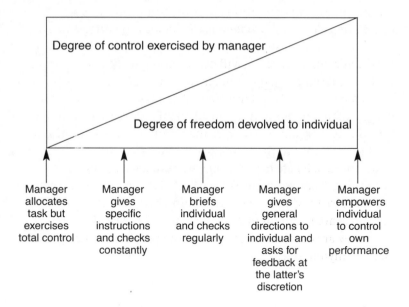

Figure 6.1   The sequence of delegation

When to delegate

You should delegate when you:

- **have more work than you can carry out yourself;**
- **cannot allow sufficient time to your priority tasks;**
- **want to develop a member of your team;**
- **believe that it will increase someone's engagement with their job;**
- **think that the job can be done adequately by the individual or the team to whom you delegate.**

What to delegate

The tasks you delegate are ones that you don't need to do yourself. You are not just ridding yourself of the difficult, tedious or unrewarding tasks. Neither are you trying simply to win for yourself an easier life. In some ways delegation will make your life more difficult, but also more rewarding.

You delegate routine and repetitive tasks which you cannot reasonably be expected to do yourself – as long as you use the time you have won productively.

You can delegate specialist tasks to those who have the skills and know-how to do them. You cannot be expected to do it all yourself. Neither can you be expected to know it all yourself. You have to know how to select and use expertise. There will be no problem as long as you make it clear what you want from the experts and get them to present it to you in a useable way. As their manager you should know what your specialists can do for you and you should be knowledgeable enough about the subject to understand whether or not what they produce is worth having.

You delegate to a team when you ask people collectively to carry out a task which you previously did yourself and which you are confident they can do.

Choosing who does the work

When delegating to individuals the person you choose to do the work should ideally have the knowledge, skills, experience, motivation and time needed to get it done to your satisfaction. It is your job as a manager or team leader to know your people – their strengths and weaknesses, what they are good at or not so good at, those who are willing to learn and those who, without good cause, think that they know it all.

Frequently you will want to delegate work to an individual who has less than the ideal experience, knowledge or skills. In these cases you should try to select someone who has intelligence, natural aptitude and, above all, willingness to learn how to do the job with help and guidance. This is how people develop, and the development of your team members should be your conscious aim whenever you delegate.

You are looking for someone you can trust. You don't want to over-supervise, so you have to believe that the person you select will get on with it and have the sense to come to you when stuck or before making a bad mistake. Of course you have to make it clear that you are there to give support and guidance when necessary, especially when a person is starting on an unfamiliar task. Initially, you may have to spend time coaching the individual to develop new or improved skills.

How do you know whom you can trust? The best way is to try people out first on smaller and less important tasks and give them more scope when they demonstrate they can do them. You may start by supervising them fairly closely but you can progressively let go until they are finally working mainly on their own with only periodic checks on progress. If they get on well, their sense of responsibility and powers of judgement will increase and improve and they will acquire the additional skills and confidence to justify your trust in their capacity to take on more demanding and responsible tasks.

Giving out the work

When you delegate you should ensure that the individuals or team concerned understand:

- **why the work needs to be done;**
- **what they are expected to do;**
- **the date by which they are expected to do it;**
- **the end-results they are expected to achieve;**
- **the authority they have to make decisions;**
- **the problems they must refer back;**
- **the progress or completion reports they should submit;**
- **any guidance and support that will be available to them.**

You have to consider how much guidance will be required on how the work should be done. You don't want to give directions in such laborious detail that you run the risk of stifling initiative. Neither do you want to infuriate people by explaining everything needlessly. As long as you are reasonably certain that they will do the job to your satisfaction without embarrassing you or seriously upsetting people, exceeding the budget or breaking the law, let them get on with it. Follow Robert Heller's golden rule: 'If you can't do something yourself, find someone who can and then let them get on with it in their own sweet way.'

You can make a distinction between hard and soft delegation. Hard delegation takes place when you tell someone exactly what to do and how to do it. You spell it out, confirm it in writing and make a note in your diary of the date when you expect the job to be completed. And then you follow up regularly.

Soft delegation takes place when you agree generally what has to be done and leave the individual to get on with it. You still agree limits of authority, define the outcomes you expect, indicate how you will review progress and lay down when exception reports should be made. An exception report is one that deals only with events out of the ordinary. It is based on the principle of management by exception, which means focusing on the key events and measures which will show up good, bad or indifferent results – the exceptions to the norm – as a guide to taking action. This approach frees people to concentrate on the issues that matter.

You should always delegate by the results you expect. When you are dealing with an experienced and capable person you don't need to specify how the results should be achieved. In the case of less experienced people you have to exercise judgement on the amount of guidance required. Newcomers with little or no experience will need plenty of guidance. They are on a 'learning curve', ie they are gradually acquiring the knowledge and skills they need to reach the required level of performance. You are responsible for seeing that they progress steadily up the learning curve, bearing in mind that everyone will be starting from a different point and learning at a different rate. It is during this period that you act as a coach or an instructor, helping people to learn and develop (see also Chapter 9). Even if you do not need to specify how the results should be achieved, it is a good idea when the delegation involves getting someone to solve a problem to ask them how they propose to solve it.

Monitoring performance

Delegation is not abdication. You are still accountable for the results obtained by the members of your team collectively and individually. The extent to which you need to monitor performance and how you do so depends on the individuals concerned and the nature of the task. If individuals or the team as a whole are inexperienced generally or are being specifically asked to undertake an unfamiliar task you may at first have to monitor performance carefully. But the sooner you can relax and watch progress informally the better. The ideal situation is when you are confident that the individual or team will deliver the results you want with the minimum of supervision. In such cases you may ask for only periodic exception reports.

For a specific task or project set target dates and keep a reminder of these in your diary so that you can check that they have been met. Don't allow people to become careless about meeting deadlines.

Without becoming oppressive, you should ensure that progress and exception reports are made when required so that you can agree any necessary corrective action. You should have indicated the extent to which people have the authority to act without reference to you. They must therefore expect to be criticized if they exceed their brief or fail to keep you informed. You don't want any surprises and your people must understand that keeping you in the dark is unacceptable.

Try to restrain yourself from interfering unnecessarily in the way the work is being done. After all, it is the results that count. Of course, you must step in if there is any danger of things going off the rails. Rash decisions, over-expenditure and ignoring defined and reasonable constraints must be prevented.

There is a delicate balance to be achieved between hedging people around with restrictions, which may appear petty, and allowing them licence to do what they like. There are no absolute rules as to where this balance should be struck. Managing people is an art not a science. But you should at least have some notion of what is appropriate based on your knowledge of the people concerned and the situation you are in. It's a judgement call but a judgement based on an understanding of the facts. The best delegators are those who have a comprehensive knowledge of the strengths and weaknesses of their team members and of the circumstances in which they work.

Above all, avoid 'river banking'. This happens when a boss gives a subordinate a task which is more or less impossible to do. As the subordinate is going down for the third time the boss can be observed in a remote and safe position on the river bank, saying: 'It's easy really, all you need to do is to try a bit harder.'

How good a delegator are you?

Check how good you are at delegating by selecting the appropriate response to the statements given in Table 6.1. Use the outcome as a basis for taking any actions you think would reduce the problem and improve your approach to delegation.

Behaviour as a delegator	Frequency of behaviour			Any action required
	Often	Occasionally	Never	
1 Do you have to take work home at night?				
2 Do you work longer hours than those you manage?				
3 Are you frequently interrupted because people come to you with questions or for advice or decisions?				
4 Do you spend part of your working time doing things for others which they could do for themselves?				
5 Do you feel that you have to keep a close watch on details if someone is to do a job right?				
6 Do you get involved in details because you enjoy them, although someone else could do them well enough?				
7 Do you lack confidence in the abilities of your team members so that you are afraid to risk them taking on more responsibility?				
8 Do you ask your people for ideas about problems that arise in their work?				
9 Do you systematically analyse and assess the abilities of your people in order to plan delegation?				
10 Do you take care to provide guidance and coaching to less experienced people so that you will be confident that you can delegate more to them?				

Table 6.1 How good are you at delegating?

7

Selection interviewing

As a manager one of your most important people management tasks will be to interview candidates for a position on your team. Even when an HR (human resources) department or a recruitment agency is involved the final decision is yours or at least shared between you and your boss. The problem is that many managers think that they are good at selecting people but aren't. This is often revealed by an analysis of leavers which shows that a large proportion leave in the first six months, about one in five according to a recent national survey. Interviewing is a skilled process and the aim of this chapter is to help you develop the skills required by first defining the nature of a selection interview and its content and then providing guidance on preparing for and planning the interview, interviewing techniques and assessing the data.

The nature of a selection interview

A selection interview should provide you with the answers to three fundamental questions:

1. Can the individual do the job? Is the person capable of doing the work to the standard required?
2. Will the individual do the job? Is the person well motivated?
3. How is the individual likely to fit into the team? Will I be able to work well with this person?

It should take the form of a conversation with a purpose. It is a conversation because candidates should be given the opportunity to talk freely about themselves and their careers. But the conversation has to be planned, directed and controlled to achieve your aims in the time available.

Your task as an interviewer is to draw candidates out to ensure that you get the information you want. Candidates should be encouraged to do most of the talking – one of the besetting sins of poor interviewers is that they talk too much. But you have to plan the structure of the interview to achieve its purpose and decide in advance the questions you need to ask – questions which will give you what you need to make an accurate assessment.

Overall, an effective approach to interviewing can be summed up as the three Cs:

- **content – the information you want and the questions you ask to get it;**
- **contact – your ability to make and maintain good contact with candidates; to establish the sort of rapport that will encourage them to talk freely, thus revealing their strengths and their weaknesses;**
- **control – your ability to control the interview so that you get the information you want.**

All this requires you to plan the interview thoroughly in terms of content, timing, structure and use of questions.

The content of an interview

The content of an interview can be analysed into three sections; its beginning, middle and end.

Beginning

At the start of the interview you should put candidates at their ease. You want them to talk freely in response to your questions. They won't do this if you plunge in too abruptly. At least welcome them and thank them for coming to the interview, expressing genuine pleasure about the meeting. But don't waste too much time talking about their journey or the weather.

Some interviewers start by describing the company and the job. Wherever possible it is best to eliminate this part of the interview by sending candidates a brief job description and something about the organization.

If you are not careful you will spend far too much time at this stage, especially if the candidate later turns out to be clearly unsuitable. A brief reference to the job should suffice and this can be extended at the end of the interview.

Middle

The middle part of the interview is where you find out what you need to know about candidates. It should take at least 80 per cent of the time, leaving, say, 5 per cent at the beginning and 15 per cent at the end.

This is when you ask questions designed to provide information on: the extent to which the knowledge, skills, capabilities and personal qualities of candidates meet the person specification; and the career history and ambitions of candidates and, sometimes, on certain aspects of their behaviour at work such as sickness and absenteeism.

End

At the end of the interview you should give candidates the opportunity to ask about the job and the company. How they do this can often give you clues about the degree to which applicants are interested and their ability to ask pertinent questions.

You may want to expand a little on the job. If candidates are promising, some interviewers at this stage extol the attractive features of the job. This is fine as long as these are not exaggerated. To give a 'realistic preview', the possible downsides should be mentioned, for example the need to travel or unsocial working hours. If candidates are clearly unsuitable you can tactfully help them to de-select themselves by referring to aspects of the work which may not appeal to them, or for which they are not really qualified. It is best not to spell out these points too strongly. It is often sufficient simply to put the question: 'This is a key requirement of the job, how do you feel about it?' You can follow up this general question by more specific questions: 'Do you feel you have the right sort of experience?' 'Are you happy about (this aspect of the job)?'

At this stage you should ask final questions about the availability of candidates, as long as they are promising. You can ask when they would be able to start and about any holiday arrangements to which they are committed.

You should also ask their permission to obtain references from their present and previous employers. They might not want you to approach their present employer and in this case you should tell them that if they are made an offer of employment it would be conditional on a satisfactory reference from their employer. It is useful to ensure that you have the names of people you can approach.

Finally, you inform candidates of what happens next. If some time could elapse before they hear from you, they should be told that you will be writing as soon as possible but that there will be some delay (don't make a promise you will be unable to keep).

It is not normally good practice to inform candidates of your decision at the end of the interview. You should take time to reflect on their suitability and you don't want to give them the impression that you are making a snap judgement.

Preparing for the interview
Initial preparations

Your first step in preparing for an interview should be to familiarize or re-familiarize yourself with the person specification, which defines the sort of individual you want in terms of qualifications, experience and personality. It is also advisable at this stage to prepare questions which you can put to all candidates to obtain the information you require. If you ask everyone some identical questions you will be able to compare the answers.

You should then read the candidates' CVs and application forms or letters. This will identify any special questions you should ask about their career or to fill in the gaps – 'what does this gap between jobs C and D signify?' (although you would not put the question as baldly as that; it would be better to say something like this: 'I see there was a gap of six months between when you left your job in C and started in D. Would you mind telling me what you were doing during this time?').

Timing

You should decide at this stage how long you want to spend on each interview. As a rule of thumb, 45 to 60 minutes are usually required for senior professional or technical appointments. Middle ranking jobs need about 30 to 45 minutes. The more routine jobs can be covered in 20 to 30 minutes. But the time allowed depends on the job and you do not want to insult a candidate by conducting a superficial interview.

Planning the interview

When planning interviews you should give some thought to how you are going to sequence your questions, especially in the middle part. There are two basic approaches as described below.

Biographical approach

The biographical approach is probably the most popular because it is simple to use and appears to be logical. The interview can be sequenced chronologically, starting with the first job or even before that at school and, if appropriate, college or university. The succeeding jobs, if any, are then dealt with in turn, ending with the present job on which most time is spent if the candidate has been in it for a reasonable time. If you are not careful, however, using the chronological method for someone who has had a number of jobs can mean spending too much time on the earlier jobs, leaving insufficient time for the most important recent experiences.

To overcome this problem, an alternative biographical approach is to start with the present job, which is discussed in some depth. The interviewer then works backwards, job by job, but concentrating only on particularly interesting or relevant experience in earlier jobs.

The problem with the biographical approach is that it is predictable. Experienced candidates are familiar with it and have their story ready, glossing over any weak points. It can also be unreliable. You can easily miss an important piece of information by concentrating on a succession of jobs rather than focusing on key aspects of the candidates' experience which illustrate their capabilities.

Criteria-based or targeted approach

This approach is based on an analysis of the person specification.

You can then select the criteria on which you will judge the suitability of the candidate, which will put you in a position to 'target' these key criteria during the interview. You can decide on the questions you need to ask to draw out from candidates information about their knowledge, skills, capabilities and personal qualities which can be compared with the criteria to assess the extent to which candidates meet the specification. This is probably the best way of focusing your interview to ensure that you get all the information you require about candidates for comparison with the person specification.

Interviewing techniques

Questioning

The most important interviewing technique you need to acquire and practise is questioning. Asking pertinent questions which elicit informative responses is a skill that people do not necessarily possess, but it is one they can develop. To improve your questioning techniques it is a good idea at the end of an interview to ask yourself: 'Did I ask the right questions?', 'Did I put them to the candidate well?', 'Did I get candidates to respond freely?'

There are a number of different types of questions as described below. By choosing the right ones you can get candidates to open up or you can pin them down to giving you specific information or to extending or clarifying a reply. The other skills you should possess are establishing rapport, listening, maintaining continuity, keeping contact and note-taking. These are considered later in this section of the chapter.

The main types of questions are described below.

Open questions

Open questions are the best ones to use to get candidates to talk – to draw them out. These are questions which cannot be

answered by a yes or no and which encourage a full response.
Single-word answers are seldom illuminating. It is a good idea to
begin the interview with one or two open questions, thus helping
candidates to settle in.

Open-ended questions or phrases inviting a response can be
phrased as follows:

- **I'd like you to tell me about the sort of work you are doing in your present job.**
- **What do you know about...?**
- **Could you give me some examples of...?**
- **In what ways do you think your experience fits you to do the job for which you have applied?**

Probing questions

Probing questions are used to get further details or to ensure
that you are getting all the facts. You ask them when answers
have been too generalized or when you suspect that there may be
some more relevant information which candidates have not
disclosed. A candidate may claim to have done something and it
may be useful to find out more about exactly what contribution
was made. Poor interviewers tend to let general and
uninformative answers pass by without probing for further
details, simply because they are sticking rigidly to a
predetermined list of open questions. Skilled interviewers are
able to flex their approach to ensure they get the facts while still
keeping control to ensure that the interview is completed on
time.

The following are some other examples of probing questions:

- **You've informed me that you have had experience in.... Could you tell me more about what you did?**
- **Could you describe in more detail the equipment you use?**
- **What training have you had to operate your machine/ equipment/computer?**
- **Why do you think that happened?**

Closed questions

Closed questions aim to clarify a point of fact. The expected reply will be an explicit single word or brief sentence. In a sense, a closed question acts as a probe but produces a succinct factual statement without going into detail. When you ask a closed question you intend to find out:

- **what the candidate has or has not done – 'What did you do then?'**
- **why something took place – 'Why did that happen?'**
- **when something took place – 'When did that happen?'**
- **how something happened – 'How did that situation arise?'**
- **where something happened – 'Where were you at the time?'**
- **who took part – 'Who else was involved?'**

Capability questions

Capability questions aim to establish what candidates know, the skills they possess and use, and what they are capable of doing. They can be open, probing or closed but they will always be focused as precisely as possible on the contents of the person specification referring to knowledge, skills and capabilities.

The sort of capability questions you can ask are:

- **What do you know about...?**
- **How did you gain this knowledge?**
- **What are the key skills you are expected to use in your work?**
- **How would your present employer rate the level of skill you have reached in...?**
- **What do you use these skills to do?**
- **How often do you use these skills?**
- **What training have you received to develop these skills?**
- **Could you please tell me exactly what sort and how much experience you have had in...?**

- Could you tell me more about what you have actually been doing in this aspect of your work?
- Can you give me any examples of the sort of work you have done which would qualify you to do this job?
- Could you tell me more about the machinery, equipment, processes or systems which you operate/for which you are responsible? (The information could refer to such aspects as output or throughput, tolerances, use of computers or software, technical problems.)
- What are the most typical problems you have to deal with?
- Would you tell me about any instances when you have had to deal with an unexpected problem or a crisis?

Unhelpful questions

There are two types of questions that are unhelpful:

- Multiple questions such as 'What skills do you use most frequently in your job? Are they technical skills, leadership skills, teamworking skills or communicating skills?' will only confuse candidates. You will probably get a partial or misleading reply. Ask only one question at a time.
- Leading questions which indicate the reply you expect are also unhelpful. If you ask a question such as: 'That's what you think, isn't it?' you will get the reply: 'Yes, I do.' If you ask a question such as: 'I take it that you don't really believe that...?' you will get the reply: 'No, I don't.' Neither of these replies will get you anywhere.

Questions to be avoided

Avoid any questions that could be construed as being biased on the grounds of sex, race, age or disability.

Ten useful questions

The following are 10 useful questions from which you can

select any that are particularly relevant in an interview you are conducting:

1. What are the most important aspects of your present job?
2. What do you think have been your most notable achievements in your career to date?
3. What sort of problems have you successfully solved recently in your job?
4. What have you learnt from your present job?
5. What has been your experience in...?
6. What do you know about...?
7. What is your approach to handling...?
8. What particularly interests you in this job and why?
9. Now you have heard more about the job, would you please tell me which aspects of your experience are most relevant?
10. Is there anything else about your career which hasn't come out yet in this interview but you think I ought to hear?

Assessing the data

If you have carried out a good interview you should have the data to assess the extent to which candidates meet each of the key points in the person specification. You can summarize your assessments by marking candidates against each of the points – 'exceeds specification', 'fully meets specification', 'just meets the minimum specification', 'does not meet the minimum specification'.

You can assess motivation broadly as 'highly motivated, 'reasonably well motivated', 'not very well motivated'.

You should also draw some conclusions from the candidate's career history and the other information you have gained about their behaviour at work. Credit should be given for a career that has progressed steadily, even if there have been several job changes. But a lot of job hopping for no good reason and without making progress can lead you to suspect that a candidate is not particularly stable.

No blame should be attached to a single setback – it can happen to anyone. But if the pattern is repeated you can reasonably be suspicious. Redundancy is not a stigma – it is happening all the time.

Finally, there is the delicate question of whether you think you will be able to work with the candidate, and whether you think he or she will fit into the team. You have to be very careful about making judgements about how you will get on with someone. But if you are absolutely certain that the chemistry will not work, then you have to take account of that feeling, as long as you ensure that you have reasonable grounds for it on the basis of the behaviour of the candidate at the interview. But be aware of the common mistakes that interviewers can make. These include:

- **jumping to conclusions on a single piece of favourable evidence – the 'halo effect';**
- **jumping to conclusions on a single piece of unfavourable evidence – the 'horns effect';**
- **not weighing up the balance between the favourable and unfavourable evidence logically and objectively;**
- **coming to firm conclusions on inadequate evidence;**
- **making snap or hurried judgements;**
- **making prejudiced judgements on the grounds of sex, race, age, disability, religion, appearance, accent, class or any aspect of the candidate's life history, circumstances or career which do not fit your preconceptions of what you are looking for.**

Coming to a conclusion

Compare your assessment of each of the candidates against one another. If any candidate fails in an area which is critical to success he or she should be rejected. You can't take a chance.

Your choice should be made between the candidates who reach an acceptable standard against each of the criteria. You can then come to an overall judgement by reference to their assessments under each heading and their career history as to which one is most likely to succeed.

In the end, your decision between qualified candidates may well be judgemental. There may be one outstanding candidate but quite often there are two or three. In these circumstances you have to come to a balanced view on which one is more likely to fit the job and the organization and have potential for a long-term career, if this is possible. Don't, however, settle for second best in desperation. It is better to try again.

Remember to make and keep notes of the reasons for your choice and why candidates have been rejected. These, together with the applications, should be kept for at least six months just in case your decision is challenged as being discriminatory.

8

Managing performance

One of your most important, if not the most important, responsibilities as a manager is to ensure that the members of your team achieve high levels of performance. You have to ensure that they understand what you expect from them, that you and they work together to review performance against those expectations and that you jointly agree what needs to be done to develop knowledge and skills and, where necessary, improve performance.

Your organization may well have a performance management system which provides guidance on how this should be done but ultimately it is up to the manager. You are the person on the spot. Performance management systems only work if managers want them to work and are capable of making them work. You have to believe that your time is well spent in the process of managing performance as described in the first part of this chapter. You need to know about performance planning (agreeing what has to be done), managing performance throughout the year and conducting formal performance reviews as covered in the next three parts. You should have no problems in appreciating the

importance of the first two activities. It is the third activity –
performance reviews – that managers often find hard to accept as
necessary and even more difficult to do well.

The process of managing performance

The process of managing performance is based on two simple
propositions. First, people are most likely to perform well when
they know and understand what is expected of them and have
taken part in defining these expectations. In other words, if you
know where you are going you are more likely to get there.
Second, the ability to meet these expectations depends on the
levels of knowledge, skill, competency and motivation of
individuals and the leadership and support they receive from
their managers.

The process takes the form of a continuous cycle as shown in
Figure 8.1. This is, in fact, the normal cycle of management.
Performance management is a natural process – it is not an
appraisal system imposed on line managers by the HR function.

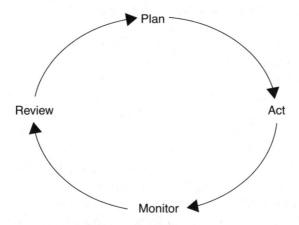

Figure 8.1   The performance management cycle

As a natural process of management, performance management involves:

1. *Planning* – reaching agreement on objectives and standards to be achieved and the level of competence to be attained; discussing and agreeing performance improvement and personal development plans.
2. *Action* – taking action to implement plans and to achieve the required standards of day-to-day work. This action is carried out by individuals with the guidance and support of their managers.
3. *Monitoring* – actions and outcomes are monitored continuously by individuals and, as necessary, by their manager (the more this can be left to individuals so that they are in effect managing their own performance, the better).
4. *Reviews* – these can take place at any appropriate time during the year. Performance management is an all-year process, not an annual event. The reviews can be quite informal, with feedback from the manager or, preferably, generated by the individual from feedback information available directly to him or her. A more formal review should take place periodically, say once or twice a year.

Performance planning

Managing performance is about getting people into action so that they achieve planned and agreed results. It focuses on what has to be done, how it should be done and what is to be achieved. But it is equally concerned with developing people – helping them to learn – and providing them with the support they need to do well, now and in the future. The framework for performance management is provided by the performance agreement, which is the outcome of performance planning. The agreement provides the basis for managing performance throughout the year and for guiding improvement and development activities. It is used as a reference point when reviewing performance and the achievement of improvement and development plans.

You should carry out performance planning jointly with the individual in order to reach agreement on what needs to be done. The starting point is the role profile which defines the results, knowledge and skills and behaviours required. This provides the basis for agreeing objectives as described below.

What are objectives?

Objectives describe something that has to be accomplished. Objectives or goals (the terms are interchangeable) define what organizations, functions, departments and individuals are expected to achieve over a period of time. Objective setting, which results in an agreement on what the role holder has to achieve, is an important part of the performance management processes of defining and managing expectations and forms the point of reference for performance reviews.

Types of objectives

The different types of objectives are described below.

Ongoing role or work objectives

All roles have built-in objectives which may be expressed as key result areas in a role profile. The definition of a key result area states that this is what the role holder is expected to achieve in this particular aspect of the role. For example: 'Identify database requirements for all projects that require data management in order to meet the needs of internal customers' or 'Deal quickly with customer queries in order to create and maintain high levels of satisfaction'.

Targets

Targets are objectives which define the quantifiable results to be attained as measured in such terms as output, through-put, income, sales, levels of service delivery, cost reduction, reduction of reject rates. Thus a customer service target could be to respond to 90 per cent of queries within two working days.

Tasks/projects

Objectives can be set for the completion of tasks or projects by a specified date or to achieve an interim result. A target for a database administrator could be to develop a new database to meet the needs of the HR department by the end of the year.

Behaviour

Behavioural expectations are often set out generally in competency frameworks which list and define the competencies which will be assessed in performance management or used for recruitment, learning and development purposes. A typical competency framework refers to the following behaviours:

- **the ability to work cooperatively and flexibly with other members of the team, with a full understanding of the role to be played as a team member;**
- **the ability to communicate clearly and persuasively, orally or in writing;**
- **the ability to manage and develop people and gain their trust and cooperation to achieve results;**
- **the exercise of unceasing care in looking after the interests of external and internal customers to ensure that their wants, needs and expectations are met or exceeded;**
- **the desire to get things done well and the ability to set and meet challenging goals, create own measures of excellence and constantly seek ways of improving performance;**

- the capacity to analyse situations, diagnose problems, identify the key issues, establish and evaluate alternative courses of action and produce a logical, practical and acceptable solution;
- the ability to decide on courses of action, ensuring that the resources required to implement the action will be available and scheduling the programme of work required to achieve a defined end-result.

Performance improvement

Performance improvement objectives define what needs to be done to achieve better results. They may be expressed in a performance improvement plan which specifies what actions need to be taken by role holders and their managers.

Learning and development

Learning and development objectives specify areas for personal development and learning in the shape of enhanced knowledge and skills. They may be recorded in a personal development plan or a learning contract as described in Chapter 9.

What is a good objective?

Many organizations state that a good objective should be 'SMART' in the sense of having the following characteristics:

S = *Specific/stretching* – clear, unambiguous, straightforward, understandable and challenging;
M = *Measurable* – quantity, quality, time, money;
A = *Achievable* – challenging but within the reach of a competent and committed person;
R = *Relevant* – relevant to the objectives of the organization so that the goal of the individual is aligned to corporate goals;
T = *Time framed* – to be completed within an agreed time-scale.

A checklist for setting SMART objectives is given below.

Objective-setting checklist

1. Has the objective-setting process been based on an agreed and up-to-date role profile which sets out key result areas?
2. Has objective setting been carried out jointly between the manager and the individual?
3. Are standards and targets clearly related to the key result areas in the role profile?
4. Do objectives support the achievement of team and corporate objectives?
5. Are the objectives specific?
6. Are they challenging?
7. Are they realistic and attainable?
8. Has a time limit for their achievement been agreed?
9. How will the achievement of objectives be measured?
10. Have any problems in attaining your objectives been identified and has action to overcome these problems been agreed?

The continuing process of managing performance

You should treat your responsibility for managing performance as an integral part of the continuing process of management. This is based on a philosophy which emphasizes:

- **the achievement of sustained improvements in performance;**

- the continuous development of skills and capabilities;
- that the organization is a 'learning organization' in the sense that it is constantly developing and applying the learning gained from experience and the analysis of the factors that have produced high levels of performance.

You should therefore be ready, willing and able to monitor performance and define and meet development and improvement needs as they arise. As far as practicable, learning and work should be integrated. This means that encouragement should be given to your team members to learn from the successes, challenges and problems inherent in their day-to-day work.

You should carry out the process of monitoring performance by reference to agreed objectives and to work, development and improvement plans. You may need only a light touch in monitoring performance if you are confident that an individual will deliver. In some cases you may have to monitor more closely. You have to decide how tightly you monitor on the basis of your understanding of the capacity of individuals to do the work. This is part of the delegation process as explained in Chapter 6.

Formal review meetings

Formal review meetings are a vital part of the process of managing performance. They provide you with the opportunity to give feedback, to sound out from individuals how they feel about their job and to plan for improvements in performance or activities to meet the learning and development needs identified during the review. The feedback will summarize and draw conclusions from what has been happening since the last review but it will be based on events and observations rather than opinion. These should have been raised at the time – there should not be any surprises during the formal discussion.

A review should take the form of a dialogue in which the two parties exchange comments and ideas and develop agreed plans. The conversation – and that is what it should be – should concentrate on analysis and review of the significant points emerging from the period under consideration. The review should be rooted in the reality of what the individual has been doing. It is concrete not abstract. It will recognize successes and identify things that have not gone according to plan in order to learn lessons for the future. It should be a joint affair – both parties are involved. So there may well be an element of self-assessment by the individuals.

A performance review meeting provides an ideal opportunity for discussing work issues away from the hurly burly of everyday working life. It can motivate people by providing a means of recognizing good performance. It can help to indicate areas in which performance needs to improve and how this should be done. And, importantly, it can help to identify learning and development needs and the means of satisfying them.

To bring the process to life, here are some of the comments made on performance reviews by team leaders in a large call centre:

- 'It gives you a structure for where you're going. You agree where you need to pick up on. It's a two-way discussion. And you're responsible for setting these objectives with your line manager. You're not just told what to do. And you go through and decide on which objectives you want to concentrate on in the next six months. It gives you a sense of responsibility for your own future.'
- 'I think you get quality time with your manager. And it's very difficult to get that time in the working environment.'
- 'The majority of my staff like the performance review. They like to know how they are doing and where they are going in the future. The ones who don't like it are those who want to do the minimum of what they can get away with.'

- 'People like feedback. They like to know how they are doing. They like to discuss their development. Even if they are not performing up to standard, they want to know how they can progress.'
- 'If you have a member of staff who is not doing so well and you sit down to talk about it, at first they say: "Well, I don't know about that." But when you give them particular instances and you talk it through, at the end of it they do say: "Well yes, you're right, I did do that." It makes them reflect positively on the negative aspects as well.'
- 'What my staff get out of it is communication. Someone is interested in what they are saying, just for once!'

Preparing for the meeting

You should initiate a formal review meeting by letting the individual know some time in advance (a week or so) when it is going to take place. Allow one or two uninterrupted hours for the meeting. The individual should be told the purpose of the meeting and the points to be covered. The aim should be, as far as possible, to emphasize the positive nature of the process and to dispel any feelings of trepidation.

The individual can then be asked to prepare for the meeting by assessing the level of performance achieved and identifying any work issues.

You should work your way through the following checklist of questions:

1. How well has the individual done in achieving agreed objectives during the review period?
2. How well have any improvement, development or training plans as agreed at the last review meeting been put into effect?
3. What should be the individual's objectives for the next review period?

4. Are you satisfied that you have given the individual sufficient guidance or help on what he/she is expected to do? If not, what extra help/guidance could you provide?
5. Is the best use being made of the individual's skills and abilities?
6. Is the individual ready to take on additional responsibilities?
7. Would the individual benefit from further experience?
8. Are there any special projects the individual could take part in which would help with his/her development?
9. What direction do you think the individual's career could take within the organization?
10. Does the individual need any further training?

Conducting a performance review meeting

In a sense a performance review is a stocktaking process answering the questions 'where have we got to?' and 'how did we get here?' But there is much more to it than that. It is not just an historical exercise, dwelling on the past and taking the form of a post mortem. The true purpose of the review is to look forward to what needs to be done by people to achieve the overall purpose of their jobs, to meet new challenges, to make even better use of their skills, knowledge and abilities and to develop their skills and competencies to further their career and increase their employability, within and outside the organization.

A constructive review meeting is most likely to take place if you:

- **encourage individuals to do most of the talking – the aim should be to conduct the meeting as a dialogue rather than using it to make 'top down' pronouncements on what you think about them;**

- listen actively to what they say;
- allow scope for reflection and analysis;
- analyse performance not personality – concentrate on what individuals have done, not the sort of people they are;
- keep the whole period under review, not concentrating on isolated or recent events;
- adopt a 'no surprises' approach – performance problems should have been identified and dealt with at the time they occurred;
- recognize achievements and reinforce strengths;
- discuss any work problems, how they have arisen and what can be done about them;
- end the meeting positively with any necessary agreed action plans (learning and development and performance improvement).

Performance review skills

The main skills you need in conducting performance reviews are asking the right questions, listening actively, providing feedback and dealing with any issues.

Asking the right questions

Only one question should be asked at a time and, if necessary, unclear responses should be played back to check understanding. The two main approaches are to use open and probe questions.

Open questions are general not specific. They provide room for people to decide how they should be answered and encourage them to talk freely. They set the scene for the more detailed analysis of performance that will follow later and can be introduced at any point to open up a discussion on a new topic. Open questions help to create an atmosphere of calm and friendly enquiry and can be expressed quite informally, for example:

- **How do you think things have been going?**
- **What do you feel about that?**
- **How can we build on that in the future?**
- **What can we learn from that?**

Open questions can be put in a 'tell me' form such as:

- **'Tell me, why do you think that happened?'**
- **'Tell me, how did you handle that situation?'**
- **'Tell me, how is this project going?'**
- **'Tell me, what do you think your key objectives are going to be next year?'**

Probe questions seek specific information on what has happened and why. They can:

- **show interest and encouragement by making supportive statements followed by questions: 'I see, and then what?'**
- **seek further information by asking 'Why?' or 'Why not?' or 'What do you mean?'**
- **explore attitudes: 'To what extent do you believe that...?'**
- **reflect views: 'Have I got the right impression, do you feel that...?'**

Listening

In a review meeting it is necessary to listen carefully. Good listeners:

- **concentrate on the speaker; they are alert at all times to the nuances of what is being said;**
- **respond quickly when appropriate but do not interrupt unnecessarily;**

- ask questions to clarify meaning;
- comment as necessary on the points made to demonstrate understanding but not at length.

Providing feedback

So far as possible, feedback on how well individuals are doing should be built into their jobs – they should have access to all the information they need to measure their own performance. But you also need to provide feedback during the performance review meeting as part of the stocktaking exercise. Here are some guidelines.

Provide feedback on actual events

Give feedback related to actual results or observed behaviour. Back it up with evidence.

Describe, don't judge

The feedback should be presented as a description of what has happened; it should not be accompanied by a judgement. If you start by saying: 'I have been informed that you have been impolite to one of our customers; we can't tolerate that sort of behaviour', you will instantly create resistance and prejudice an opportunity to encourage improvement.

Refer to specific behaviours

Relate all your feedback to specific items of behaviour. Don't indulge in transmitting general feelings or impressions.

Ask questions

Ask questions rather than make statements – 'Why do you think this happened?'; 'On reflection, is there any other way in which you think you could have handled the situation?'; 'How do you think you should tackle this sort of situation in the future?'.

Select key issues

Select key issues and restrict yourself to them. There is a limit to how much criticism anyone can take. If you overdo it, the shutters will go up and you will get nowhere.

Focus

Focus on aspects of performance the individual can improve. It is a waste of time to concentrate on areas that the individual can do little or nothing about.

Provide positive feedback

Provide feedback on the things that the individual did well in addition to areas for improvement. People are more likely to work positively at improving their performance and developing their skills if they feel empowered by the process.

Dealing with issues

In a review meeting you have to deal with performance issues. Some will be positive, others may be negative. Dealing with negative points is often the area of greatest concern to line managers, many of whom do not like handing out criticisms. But this is not what performance reviews are about. They should not be regarded simply as an opportunity for attaching blame for something that has gone wrong in the past. If there has been a problem it should have been discussed when it happened. But this does not mean that persistent under-performance should go unnoticed during the review meeting. Specific problems may have been dealt with at the time but it may still be necessary to discuss a pattern of under-performance. The first step, and often the most difficult one, is to get people to agree that there is room for improvement. This will best be achieved if the discussion focuses on factual evidence of performance problems. Some people will never admit to being wrong and in those cases you may have to say in effect: 'Here is the evidence; I have no doubt that this is correct; I am afraid you have to accept from me on the basis of this evidence that your performance in this respect has been unsatisfactory.'

And the positive elements should not be neglected. Too often they are overlooked or mentioned briefly then put on one side. Avoid a sequence of comments like this:

- **objective number one – fantastic;**
- **objective number two – that was great;**
- **objective number three – couldn't have been done better;**
- **now objective number four – this is what we really need to talk about, what went wrong?**

If this sort of approach is adopted, the discussion will focus on the failure, the negatives, and the individual will become defensive. This can be destructive and explains why some people feel that the annual review meeting is going to be a 'beat me over the head' session or part of a blame culture.

To under-emphasize the positive aspects reduces the scope for action and motivation. More can be achieved by building on success than by concentrating on failure. In the words of Bing Crosby: 'Accentuate the positive, eliminate the negative.'

9

Helping people to learn and develop

As a manager or team leader you need skilled, knowledgeable and competent people in your department or team. You may appoint able people from within and outside the organization but most of them will still have a lot to learn about their jobs. And to improve your team members' performance you must not only ensure that they learn the basic skills they need but also that they develop those skills to enable them to perform even better when faced with new demands and challenges.

Most learning happens at the place of work, although it can be supplemented by such activities as e-learning (the delivery of learning opportunities and support via computer, networked and web-based technology) and formal 'off-the-job' training courses. It is your job to ensure that favourable conditions for learning 'on the job' exist generally in your area as well as taking steps to help individuals develop. To do this job well you need to know about:

- **the conditions that enable effective learning to take place;**
- **the importance of 'self-managed learning', ie individuals taking control of their own learning;**

- the contribution of formal learning;
- the advantages and disadvantages of informal learning and development approaches;
- how you can contribute to promoting learning and development in your department or team;
- the use of such learning and development aids as coaching, mentoring, learning contracts and personal development plans;
- how to instruct people in specific tasks should the need arise.

Conditions for effective learning

The conditions required for learning to be effective are:

- Individuals must be motivated to learn. They should be aware that their present level of knowledge, skill or competence, or their existing attitude or behaviour, needs to be developed or improved if they are to perform their work to their own and to others' satisfaction. They must, therefore, have a clear picture of the behaviour they should adopt.
- Good learning is more likely to be achieved if learners have learning goals. They should have targets and standards of performance which they find acceptable and achievable and can use to judge their own progress. They should be encouraged and helped to set their own goals.
- Learners need a sense of direction and feedback on how they are doing. Self-motivated individuals may provide much of this for themselves, but guidance, help and encouragement should still be available when necessary – they should not be left to sink or swim.
- Learners must gain satisfaction from learning. They are most capable of learning if it satisfies one or more of

their needs. Conversely, the best learning programmes can fail if they are not seen as useful by those undertaking them.

- Learning is an active, not a passive process. Learners need to be actively involved.
- Appropriate processes and methods should be used. A large repertory of these exists but they must be used with discrimination in accordance with the needs and learning style of the individual and the group.
- Learning methods should be varied. The use of a variety of methods, as long as they are all appropriate, helps learning by engaging the interest of learners.
- Learning requires time to assimilate, test and accept. This time should be provided in the learning programme.
- The learner should receive reinforcement of correct behaviour. Learners usually need to know quickly that they are doing well. In a prolonged programme, intermediate steps are required in which learning can be reinforced.
- It must be recognized that there are different levels of learning and that these need different methods and take different times. At the simplest level, learning requires direct physical responses, memorization and basic conditioning. At a higher level, learning involves adapting existing knowledge or skill to a new task or environment. At the next level, learning becomes a complex process when principles are identified in a range of practices or actions, when a series of isolated tasks have to be integrated or when the process is about developing interpersonal skills. The most complex form of learning takes place when learning is concerned with the values and attitudes of people and groups.
- The focus should be on individual learning, ensuring that it takes place when required – ' just-for-you' and 'just-in-time' learning.

Self-managed learning

Self-managed learning involves encouraging individuals to take responsibility for their own learning needs. The aim is to encourage 'discretionary learning', which happens when individuals actively seek to acquire the knowledge and skills required to perform well. It is based on processes of recording achievement and action planning, which involves individuals reviewing what they have learnt, what they have achieved, what their goals are, how they are going to achieve those goals and what new learning they need to acquire. The learning programme can be 'self-paced' in the sense that learners can decide for themselves, up to a point, the rate at which they work and are encouraged to measure their own progress and adjust the programme accordingly.

Self-directed learning is based on the principle that people learn and retain more if they find things out for themselves. But they still need to be given guidance on what to look for and help in finding it. Learners have to be encouraged to define, with whatever help they may require, what they need to know to perform their job effectively. They need to be provided with guidance on where they can get the material or information that will help them to learn and how to make good use of it. Personal development plans as described later in this chapter can provide a framework for this process. People also need support from their manager and the organization, with the provision of coaching, mentoring and learning facilities, including e-learning.

Formal learning

Formal learning is planned and systematic and involves the use of structured approaches to learning. It may be provided by the organization in the form of training courses and you need to know what is available and its relevance to the learning needs of your team members. However, people are too often sent on company courses 'because they are there'. Such courses should only be used if they are relevant. You should be confident that the learning acquired on the course is needed by the people involved and can be transferred to the place of work, which is not always the case. Informal learning which is under your direct control, is rooted in the work people do and is continuous and progressive can be much more appropriate.

Informal learning

Informal learning is learning through experience. For many people learning takes place entirely in the workplace while they are doing their normal job. The simple act of observing more experienced colleagues can accelerate learning; conversing, swapping stories, cooperating on tasks and offering mutual support deepen and solidify the process. This kind of learning – often very informal in nature – is thought by many learning and development experts to be vastly more effective in building proficiency than more formalized training methods.

The advantages of informal learning are that it is relevant – it takes place in the working environment. Understanding can be achieved in incremental steps rather than in indigestible hunks and learners can readily put their learning into practice.

The disadvantages are that it may be left to chance – some people will benefit, some won't. It can be unplanned and unsystematic and learners may simply pick up bad habits. These disadvantages are significant. You cannot leave learning to chance; as explained below, you have a vital part to play.

How you can promote learning and development

Overall your role is to ensure that conditions in your department or team are conducive to learning. This can be described as creating a 'learning culture', an environment in which steps are taken to understand how learning can benefit individual and team performance, to provide learning opportunities as the need arises, to encourage self-managed learning and to recognize that learning is a continuous process in which all can take part and everyone can benefit. Your function is to provide the leadership and example that will foster this culture and to see that guidance and help are available from you and others to promote learning and development. To do this you must understand learning needs, provide for induction training, use day-to-day contacts with people to provide them with learning opportunities, and prepare and agree learning contracts and personal development plans. You must also be familiar with the various techniques or processes involved, namely coaching, mentoring and job instruction.

Understanding learning needs

You should be aware of the knowledge and skills required to carry out each job in your team so that you can plan the learning programme required for new team members and review the levels reached by existing team members to identify any further learning needs. The basis for this should be role profiles, as described in Chapter 4, which spell out the knowledge and skill required to reach an acceptable level of performance. You can then draw up specifications of what people should learn and how they should learn it.

If there are learning and development professionals in your organization they can help you to carry out analyses and prepare learning plans. For key jobs a learning specification can be produced as shown in Figure 9.1.

Induction training

You are initially involved in helping people to learn every time you welcome new members of your team, plan how they are

LEARNING SPECIFICATION	
Role title: Product Manager	**Department:** Marketing
What the role holder must understand	
Learning outcomes	***Learning methods***
● The product market ● The product specification ● Market research availability ● Interpretation of marketing data ● Customer service requirements ● Techniques of product management	● Briefing by marketing manager and advertising manager ● Briefing by operations manager ● Briefing by market research manager ● Coaching: market research manager ● Briefing by customer service manager ● Institute of Marketing courses
What the role holder must be able to do	
Learning outcomes	***Learning methods***
● Prepare product budget ● Prepare marketing plans ● Conduct market reviews ● Prepare marketing campaigns ● Specify requirements for advertisements and promotional material ● Liaise with advertising agents and creative suppliers ● Analyse results of advertising campaigns ● Prepare marketing reports	● Coaching by budget accountant ● Coaching by mentor ● Coaching by market research manager ● Read product manager's manual ● Read product manager's manual ● Attachment to agency ● Coaching by mentor ● Read previous reports, observe marketing review meetings, coaching by mentor

Figure 9.1   A learning specification

going to acquire the know-how required (preferably as recorded in a learning specification), provide for them to receive systematic guidance and instruction on the tasks they have to carry out and see that the plan is implemented. As a manager you may delegate the responsibility for providing this induction training to a team leader, or as a team leader you may carry it out yourself – the ideal method – or delegate it to a team member. Whichever approach you use, you should be confident that the individual responsible for the induction has the right temperament and skills to do it. This includes being aware of the conditions required for effective learning as set out earlier and of the use of coaching, mentoring and job instruction as described later.

Continuous learning

You provide learning opportunities for team members every time you delegate tasks to them. At the briefing stage you ensure that they are fully aware of what they have to do and have the knowledge and skills to do it. If appropriate, you ask them to tell you what they need to know and be able to do to carry out the task. If you are unsure that they have all the skills required but still believe that they can do it with additional guidance or help, then this is what you provide yourself or arrange for someone else to do.

As you monitor progress to whatever degree is necessary (for some people you will just let them get on with it; for less experienced people you might need to monitor more closely), you can follow up to find out if the best approach is being used and if not, give them any further help they need. But you must be careful. People will not learn if you do it all for them. You have to give them a chance to find things out for themselves and even make mistakes as long as things are not going badly wrong.

When you review outcomes with people, preferably immediately after the event, it is a good idea to ask them what they have learnt so that it is reinforced for future use. You can also ask them if their experience has shown that they need to learn. This is a good opportunity for you to get individuals to develop their own learning plans (self-managed learning) but it also means that you can step in and offer your support.

Learning contracts

A learning contract is a formal agreement between the manager and the individual on what learning needs to take place, the objectives of such learning and what part the individual, the manager, the learning and development department (if one exists) or a mentor will play in ensuring that learning happens. The partners to the contract agree on how the objectives will be achieved and their respective roles. It will spell out learning programmes and indicate what coaching, mentoring and formal training activities should be carried out. It is, in effect, a blueprint for learning. Learning contracts can be part of a personal development planning process as described below.

Personal development planning

Personal development planning is carried out by individuals with guidance, encouragement and help from you as required. A personal development plan sets out the actions people propose to take to learn and to develop themselves. They take responsibility for formulating and implementing the plan but they receive support from their managers in doing so.

The stages of personal development planning are modelled in Figure 9.2. The content of each stage is described below:

1. *Analyse current situation and development needs*. This can be done as part of a performance management process.
2. *Set goals*. These could include improving performance in the current job, improving or acquiring skills, extending relevant knowledge, developing specified areas of competence, moving across or upwards in the organization, preparing for changes in the current role.
3. *Prepare action plan*. The action plan sets out what needs to be done and how it will be done under headings such as outcomes expected (learning objectives), the development activities, the responsibility for development (what

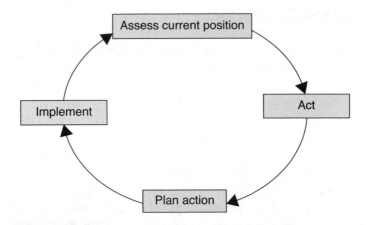

Figure 9.2   Stages in preparing and implementing a personal development plan

individuals are expected to do and the support they will get from their manager, the HR department or other people), and timing. A variety of activities tuned to individual needs should be included in the plan; for example: observing what others do, project work, planned use of e-learning programmes and internal learning resource centres, working with a mentor, coaching by the line manager or team leader, experience in new tasks, guided reading and special assignments. Formal training to develop knowledge and skills may be part of the plan but it is not the most important part.

4.   *Implement*. Take action as planned.

The plan can be expressed in the form of a learning contract.

Coaching

Coaching is a one-to-one method of helping people develop their skills and competencies. Coaching is often provided by specialists from inside or outside the organization who concentrate on specific areas of skills or behaviour, for example leadership. But it is also something that can happen in the workplace. As a manager or team leader you should be prepared and able to act as a coach when necessary to see that learning takes place.

The need for coaching may arise from formal or informal performance reviews, but opportunities for coaching emerge during day-to-day activities. As part of the normal process of management, coaching consists of:

- **making people aware of how well they are performing by, for example, asking them questions to establish the extent to which they have thought through what they are doing;**
- **controlled delegation – ensuring that individuals not only know what is expected of them but also understand what they need to know and be able to do to complete the task satisfactorily; this gives managers an opportunity to provide guidance at the outset – guidance at a later stage may be seen as interference;**
- **using whatever situations may arise as opportunities to promote learning;**
- **encouraging people to look at higher-level problems and how they would tackle them.**

A common framework used by coaches is the GROW model:

'G' is for the goal of coaching, which needs to be expressed in specific measurable terms that represent a meaningful step towards future development.

'R' is for the reality check – the process of eliciting as full as possible a description of what the person being coached needs to learn.

'O' is for option generation – the identification of as many solutions and actions as possible.

'W' is for wrapping up – when the coach ensures that the individual being coached is committed to action.

To succeed in coaching you need to understand that your role is to help people to learn and see that they are motivated to learn. They should be aware that their present level of knowledge or skill or their behaviour needs to be improved if they are going to perform their work satisfactorily. Individuals should be given guidance on what they should be learning and feedback on how they are doing, and, because learning is an active not a passive process, they should be actively involved with you in your role as a coach who should be constructive, building on strengths and experience.

Coaching may be informal but it has to be planned. It is not simply checking from time to time on what people are doing and then advising them on how to do it better. Nor is it occasionally telling people where they have gone wrong and throwing in a lecture for good measure. As far as possible, coaching should take place within the framework of a general plan of the areas and direction in which individuals will benefit from further development. Coaching plans can and should be incorporated into the personal development plans set out in a performance agreement.

Coaching should provide motivation, structure and effective feedback. As a coach, you should believe that people can succeed and that they can contribute to their own success.

Mentoring

Mentoring is the process of using specially selected and trained individuals to provide guidance, pragmatic advice and continuing support which will help the person or persons allocated to them to learn and develop. It can be regarded as a method of helping people to learn, as distinct from coaching, which is a relatively directive means of increasing people's competence.

Mentoring involves learning on the job, which must always be the best way of acquiring the particular skills and knowledge the job holder needs. It also complements formal training by providing those who benefit from it with individual guidance from experienced managers who are 'wise in the ways of the organization'.

Mentors provide people with:

- **advice in drawing up self-development programmes or learning contracts;**
- **general help with learning programmes;**
- **guidance on how to acquire the necessary knowledge and skills to do a new job;**
- **advice on dealing with any administrative, technical or people problems individuals meet, especially in the early stages of their careers;**
- **information on 'the way things are done around here' – the corporate culture in terms of expected behaviour;**
- **coaching in specific skills;**
- **help in tackling projects – not by doing it for them but by pointing them in the right direction; helping people to help themselves;**
- **a parental figure with whom individuals can discuss their aspirations and concerns and who will lend a sympathetic ear to their problems.**

Mentors are people who are likely to adopt the right non-directive but supportive help to the person or persons they are dealing with. They must then be carefully briefed and trained in their role.

As a manager you may be asked to act as a mentor and you should receive guidance on what is involved. But you may be able to call on an organizational mentor to provide help with an individual in your area.

A version of mentoring which you can use within your department is what in the United States is sometimes called 'buddying'. This involves appointing someone in your department or team to look after newcomers and ensure that they get the guidance and help they need to settle down quickly.

Job instruction

When you arrange for people to learn specific tasks, especially those involving manual skills, the learning will be more effective if you use, or arrange for someone to use, job instruction techniques. The sequence of instruction should consist of the following stages.

Preparation

Preparation for each instruction period means that the trainer must have a plan for presenting the subject matter and using appropriate teaching methods, visual aids and demonstration aids. It also means preparing trainees for the instruction that is to follow. They should want to learn. They must perceive that the learning will be relevant and useful to them personally. They should be encouraged to take pride in their job and to appreciate the satisfaction that comes from skilled performance.

Presentation

Presentation should consist of a combination of telling and showing – explanation and demonstration. Explanation should be as simple and direct as possible: the trainer explains briefly the ground to be covered and what to look for. He or she makes the maximum use of charts, diagrams and other visual aids. The aim should be to teach first things first and then proceed from the known to the unknown, the simple to the complex, the concrete to the abstract, the general to the particular, the observation to reasoning, and the whole to the parts and back to the whole again.

Demonstration

Demonstration is an essential stage in instruction, especially when the skill to be learnt is mainly a doing skill. Demonstration can take place in three stages:

1. The complete operation is shown at normal speed to show the trainee how the task should be carried out eventually.
2. The operation is demonstrated slowly and in correct sequence, element by element, to indicate clearly what is done and the order in which each task is carried out.
3. The operation is demonstrated again slowly, at least two or three times, to stress the how, when and why of successive movements.

The learner then practises by imitating the instructor and constantly repeating the operation under guidance. The aim is to reach the target level of performance for each element of the total task, but the instructor must constantly strive to develop coordinated and integrated performance; that is, the smooth combination of the separate elements of the task into a whole job pattern.

Follow-up

Follow-up continues during the training period for all the time required by the learner to reach a level of performance equal to that of the normal experienced worker in terms of quality, speed and attention to safety. During the follow-up stage, the learner will continue to need help with particularly difficult tasks or to overcome temporary setbacks which result in a deterioration of performance. The instructor may have to repeat the presentation of the elements and supervise practice more closely until the trainee regains confidence or masters the task.

10

Rewarding people

People will contribute more and cooperate more wholeheartedly if they feel that they are valued. This happens when you recognize them for what they achieve and reward them according to their contribution. Although many organizations have some form of reward system, usually managed by the HR function, it is the frontline manager who exerts the greatest influence on how people are valued. The extent to which line managers are responsible for rewarding people varies according to the system used or the lack of a system. Managers in public and many voluntary sector organizations exert little influence on the financial aspects of reward. There will be a pay spine with fixed increments related to service and, probably, a job evaluation scheme which dictates job gradings and therefore pay. However, in many small or even medium-sized organizations there is no formal reward system and managers have a considerable degree of freedom in managing pay.

Reference has been made above to 'reward systems' and if you are working in an organization with one, it is necessary to understand what this term means, and this is explained in the first part of the chapter. The overall approach you should adopt to rewarding people, whether or not there is a system, is discussed in the next part. The following parts of the chapter are concerned with what managers and team leaders do about deciding on grades and rates for the job, and with conducting pay reviews when systems exist for progressing pay according to performance or contribution. The last part of the chapter covers what managers do when there is no reward system or only a vestigial one.

Reward systems

A reward system consists of explicit policies, practices and procedures which are organized and managed as a whole. A complete system is based on reward policies which set guidelines for decision making and action. For example, an organization may have a policy which sets the levels of pay in the organization compared with median market rates. The system itself consists of reward practices which comprise grading jobs, deciding on rates of pay and reviewing pay levels, grade and pay structures, methods of progressing pay according to performance, contribution or service, and employee benefits such as pension schemes and sick pay. The degree to which these practices are formalized will vary considerably between different organizations. For example, many organizations (60 per cent according to a recent e-reward survey) have formal job evaluation schemes, but a large proportion rely on more or less informal methods. Similarly, a lot of organizations have formal grade and pay structures but 20 per cent of those responding to the e-reward survey had no structure at all. And performance and contribution-related pay schemes vary enormously in the ways in which they operate.

The implication is that if you want to play your part in managing the reward system you must understand how it works. You should be told this by HR but, if not, it's up to you to find out.

Approaches to rewarding people

You need to understand the factors that determine the effectiveness of the formal or informal system in terms of the degree to which it satisfies people because they feel valued and the extent to which it contributes to their motivation and engagement. These factors consist of the use of both financial and non-financial rewards and how the system is operated as a fair, equitable, consistent and transparent approach to rewarding people.

Financial and non-financial rewards

Financial rewards consist of the rate for the job (base pay), pay related to performance or contribution (contingent pay) and benefits such as pension schemes. The ways such rewards work as motivators were considered in Chapter 3. To be effective, such rewards should be perceived as fair, equitable and consistent (see below). They will work better if the system is transparent. People should also expect that their efforts will lead to a worthwhile reward – there must be a 'line of sight' between what they do and what they get, between the effort and the reward. They will also respond more to financial rewards if the system is transparent – they know how it works and how it affects them.

Non-financial rewards can provide a better basis for valuing people because they are more under your control. You are in the best position to value people through them. Financial rewards are restricted by financial budgets and company procedures. The main ways of valuing people through non-financial rewards are:

- **providing them with the opportunity to achieve;**
- **recognizing their contribution by praise and by 'applause' (letting others know how well you value an individual);**
- **giving people more responsibility (empowering them);**

- providing them with the opportunity to grow – offering learning opportunities, encouraging and supporting the preparation and implementation of personal development plans and broadening their experience (job enlargement).

Both financial and non-financial rewards are important. Many organizations are now combining their impact by developing what is called a 'total reward' system. Essentially, this notion of total reward says that there is more to rewarding people than throwing money at them. Unilever states that total reward 'encompasses all the elements that make it worthwhile for people to come to work'. Perhaps the most powerful argument for a total rewards approach was produced by Professor Jeffrey Pfeffer (1998) of Stanford University:

> Creating a fun, challenging, and empowered work environment in which individuals are able to use their abilities to do meaningful jobs for which they are shown appreciation is likely to be a more certain way to enhance motivation and performance – even though creating such an environment may be more difficult and take more time than simply turning the reward lever.

Fairness

People will react positively to financial rewards if they feel that they are fair – this is the 'felt-fair' principle. Perceptions on fairness are based on the extent to which people believe that the procedure followed in making the reward is fair and they are rewarded according to their desserts. If there is a performance-related pay system they will want to feel that the method of assessing their performance was based on what they had actually achieved and was not affected by bias, prejudice or ignorance. They will also want to feel that their rewards are commensurate with their performance compared with other people, ie they are equitable, as discussed below.

Equity

Equity is achieved when people are rewarded appropriately in relation to others within the organization and in accordance with their worth and the value of their contribution. An equitable reward system ensures that relative worth is measured as objectively as possible and that a framework is provided for making defensible judgements about job values and grading.

Consistent

The system should allow consistent decisions to be made about reward levels and individual rates of pay. Policy guidelines should be available to line managers to ensure that they avoid making decisions that deviate unjustifiably from what would be generally regarded as fair and equitable.

Transparent

Transparency exists in a reward system when people understand how reward processes function and how they are affected by them. The reasons for pay decisions are explained at the time they are made. Employees have a voice in the development of reward policies and practices.

The role of managers

You are in a strong position to make the difference in all these areas. But remember that if you want people to be more motivated and engaged because they feel more valued, it is deeds not words that count. Inconsistency between what is said and done is the best way to undermine trust and generate employee cynicism, lack of interest or even open hostility.

Fixing grades and rates of pay

If there is a grade and pay structure, those parts of the organization's reward system in the form of its job evaluation scheme and its procedures for analysing market rates largely determine how jobs are graded and the basic rates for jobs. You can influence decisions about individuals by invoking the job evaluation scheme to grade or re-grade jobs and by scanning any information on market rates that you think justifies more pay for someone.

Job evaluation procedures are based on job descriptions which highlight the characteristics of the job with respect to any factors used in the scheme, such as the levels of skill and responsibility involved. In point-factor schemes (the most common method) judgements about these levels are converted into points so that a total score is attached to a job which determines its grade and therefore pay. Managers are often tempted to advance the cause of their staff by inflating the characteristics set out in the job description and therefore committing the sin of 'point grabbing'. This is undesirable because a) it is dishonest, b) it damages the integrity of the scheme and c) it creates inequities between jobs.

One of the issues that should concern you is that of equal pay for work of equal value. Your aim should be to achieve equity between like jobs held by men or women, people in different racial groups, sexual orientation or religion, people with and without disabilities and older and younger people. This will avoid expensive and time-consuming equal pay cases but, more importantly, it is the right thing to do.

Reviewing pay

Decisions on general 'across the board' increases are generally outside the line manager's control. But if your organization has a scheme for relating individual pay to performance or contribution you will be involved in determining the amounts people should get. In the past, line managers were often given little scope to make such decisions and even the extent to which they could influence them was limited. Increasingly, however, responsibility is being devolved to managers and this makes quite considerable demands on their judgement and their ability to be fair and consistent. One of the reasons why most unions oppose performance-related pay is that they believe, not without some justification, that managers tend to be unfair and prone to prejudice and favouritism when, as part of a performance appraisal scheme, they rate performance on a scale that governs pay increases.

Either that, or managers can play a zero sum game by awarding a few high increases to their favourites and keeping within their budgets by distributing small awards to other people or nothing at all. Alternatively, they can fail to discriminate between performance levels by awarding everyone, or at least the vast majority of people, the same. Managers in a public sector government agency once torpedoed a performance-related pay scheme they didn't like by giving everyone the same 'box markings', ie performance ratings, which meant that all the staff got the same small increase.

Some organizations have addressed these issues by devolving pay to line managers but ensuring that they are issued with guidelines and technical support in making pay decisions. For example, the HR function at Lloyds TSB traditionally controlled the implementation of pay policies and practices. Line managers did what they were told. The company gradually replaced these centralized, command and control arrangements with a system of devolved pay management. As Tim Fevyer, Senior Manager, Compensation and Benefits, explained: 'Lloyds TSB considered that the best place for making decisions about people's basic pay is where the majority of information is. Most of the information, skills and knowledge is held at the local level with the line manager. Rather than dictate pay adjustments from the centre pay management decisions were devolved. Line managers were given a pot of money and were free to allocate it where the need was greatest and where circumstances dictate.' The broad guidelines provided by Lloyds TSB to line managers suggested that in making pay decisions they should consider:

- **the individual's current role and pay position in the salary range;**
- **what people in the same or similar roles are being paid;**
- **how they value the individual's skills, competencies and performance in this role, relative to the nearest pay reference point;**
- **the function and geographical market rate for this role;**
- **what recent pay awards they have received;**
- **entering into a 'dialogue' about expectations – managers should talk to their people about where they are and where they could be;**
- **any other relevant factors such as the degree of challenge of the job, the amount of learning required, and their recent performance history.**

Line managers are now provided with a pay pot, which could be worth, say, 3.5 per cent of the pay budget, and are free to distribute it to reflect each individual's contribution. They are supplied with details of the salaries they would be expected to pay a typical employee who is fully experienced and consistently delivers a fully effective level of performance over a sustained period of time in a given role. Additionally, managers are supplied with details of actual salaries in their department or area to enable them to make comparisons against the relevant internal market. They are also given the pay reference points for the appropriate benchmark roles. An individual may be paid at, below or above this pay reference point, depending on the contribution of their role relative to the nearest benchmark role, and on their experience, skills and contribution in their particular role. Pay decisions are made on the basis of the manager's overall budget pay pot, the market, and internal equity, and they are scrutinized by the manager's manager and the HR manager for fairness and consistency. There is a need to exercise control to achieve what is regarded as a proper degree of equity and consistency. Besides adherence to the pay budget, additional control is provided by careful monitoring of the distribution of pay in bands to ensure that anomalies and unusual pay distributions do not occur. But the structure provides line managers with much greater flexibility to manage the career development and pay of their staff.

Many organizations try to avoid the problems of relying on performance ratings in the annual performance review to inform pay decisions, largely because this process runs counter to the main objective of such reviews, which is to improve performance and to provide the basis for learning and development plans. Quite often, such organizations 'decouple' pay reviews from performance reviews, ie they hold them at separate times in the year, possibly three or four months apart. They may even abandon ratings altogether and simply ask managers to recommend above average, average or below average pay increases depending on their assessments of contribution, potential market rate relativities and the rates of pay of other team members. To help managers they provide them with systems support. For example, a financial sector company purchased a software application which helps it to develop an in-depth compensation reward modelling capability and put more decisions in the hands of line managers. The pay review modelling software enables the company to create performance guidelines which are issued to line managers and generate reports analysing the distribution of pay by almost any variable, to assist in managing and auditing the reward system. These reports are standardized across the business and provided to the managers responsible for pay decisions. Spreadsheets can be developed, as at Bass Brewers, which provide managers with the data they need on the distribution of pay amongst their staff and on market rates. They enable them to model alternative distributions of awards and, after a series of 'what ifs', achieve the optimum distribution of their pay review budget to individuals.

Managing without a reward system

If you do not have the support of a formal reward system or a helpful HR department, you may largely have to make decisions yourself on what people should be paid. You may have to get approval from a higher authority and you may have to work within a budget, but you are virtually on your own when you deal with your staff. In these circumstances there are 10 things you should do as set out below.

Managing your own reward system

1. Remember that you are attempting to achieve internal equity (paying people according to their relative contribution) at the same time as being externally competitive (paying rates that will attract and retain the level of people you need).
2. Appreciate that it is often difficult to reconcile equity and competitiveness.
3. Obtain information on market rates from reliable sources (surveys and agencies). Do not rely on job advertisements.
4. If you have to bow to market forces, make certain that you have got your facts right and that the case for what is sometimes called a market supplement can be objectively justified.
5. Take steps to ensure that equal pay is provided for work of equal value.
6. Try to obtain objective reasons differentiating between the base pay of different jobs. While you need not go to the extreme of developing your own analytical job evaluation scheme, you can at least compare jobs by

reference to role profiles which indicate the levels of responsibility and knowledge and skills they involve.

7. Review rates basic of pay by reference to market rates, not just to increases in the cost of living.

8. When looking at individual rates of pay, consider what people are earning in relation to their colleagues. Ask yourself the questions: are they just as good, are they better, are they worse than their colleagues? Rank your team members in order by reference to their relative levels of contribution. Give the top 15% or so an above average increase, the bottom 15% or so a below average increase and the rest an average increase.

9. Consider other methods of rewarding your people besides pay, especially recognizing their contribution.

10. Ensure that your team members know the basis upon which you have made decisions about their pay and give them the opportunity to raise any of their concerns.

11

Managing change

Change is the only constant thing that happens in organizations. There can be few managers who have never had to meet the challenge of introducing a new organization structure, new methods of working, a revision to job duties, new management systems or alterations in terms and conditions of employment.

The challenge arises because people can find change difficult to accept or to cope with. Many people resist change, any change. Some may accept the need for change but can't adjust their behaviour to respond to it. There are some people who welcome change but they are probably in the minority.

Your role as a manager is to see that change happens smoothly when the occasion arises. To do this you should know the general approaches you can take to manage change, the reasons why people resist change and how to overcome this resistance, and the specific steps you can take to introduce change and ensure that it takes place as planned.

Approaches to managing change

The following five approaches to managing change were identified by Professor Keith Thurley (1979) of the London School of Economics:

1. *Directive* – the imposition of change in crisis situations or when other methods have failed. This is done by the exercise of managerial power without consultation.
2. *Bargained* – this approach recognizes that power is shared between the employer and the employed and that change requires negotiation, compromise and agreement before being implemented.
3. *'Hearts and minds'* – an all-embracing thrust to change the attitudes, values and beliefs of the whole workforce. This seeks 'commitment' and 'shared vision' but does not necessarily include involvement or participation.
4. *Analytical* – an approach to change which proceeds sequentially from the analysis and diagnosis of the situation, through the setting of objectives, the design of the change process, the evaluation of the results and, finally, the determination of the objectives for the next stage in the change process. This is the rational and logical approach much favoured by consultants – external and internal. But change seldom proceeds as smoothly as this model would suggest. Emotions, power politics and external pressures mean that the rational approach, although it might be the right way to start, is difficult to sustain.
5. *Action-based* – this recognizes that the way managers behave in practice bears little resemblance to the analytical model. The distinction between managerial thought and managerial action blurs in the event to the point of invisibility. What managers think is what they do. Real life therefore often results in a 'ready, aim, fire' approach to change management. This typical approach to change

starts with a broad belief that some sort of problem exists, although it may not be well defined. The identification of possible solutions, often on a trial and error basis, leads to a clarification of the nature of the problem and a shared understanding of a possible optimal solution, or at least a framework within which solutions can be discovered.

The analytical process may be ideal and should at least be attempted. But it should be tempered with the realism attached to the action-based approach.

Resistance to change

Change management programmes have to take account of the fact that many people resist change. There are those who are stimulated by change and see it as a challenge and an opportunity. But they are in the minority. It is always easy for people to select any of the following 10 reasons for doing nothing:

1. It won't work.
2. We're already doing it.
3. It's been tried before without success.
4. It's not practical.
5. It won't solve the problem.
6. It's too risky.
7. It's based on pure theory.
8. It will cost too much.
9. It will antagonize the customers/management/the union/ the workers/the shareholders.
10. It will create more problems than it solves.

Reasons for resistance to change

People resist change when they see it as a threat to their established life at work. They are used to their routines and patterns of behaviour and may be concerned about their ability to cope with new demands. They see change as a threat to familiar patterns of behaviour. They may believe that it will affect their status, security or their earnings. Sometimes, and with good reason, they may not believe statements by management that the change is for their benefit as well as that of the organization. They may feel that managements have ulterior motives and sometimes, the louder management protests, the less it will be believed.

Joan Woodward (1968) looked at change from the viewpoint of employees and wrote:

> When we talk about resistance to change we tend to imply that management is always rational in changing its direction, and that employees are stupid, emotional or irrational in not responding in the way they should. But if an individual is going to be worse off, explicitly or implicitly, when the proposed changes have been made, any resistance is entirely rational in terms of their best interest. The interests of the organization and the individual do not always coincide.

Overcoming resistance to change

Because resistance to change is a natural and even inevitable phenomenon it may be difficult to overcome. But the attempt must be made. This starts with an analysis of the likely effect of change and the extent to which it might be resisted, by whom and why. It is not enough to think out what the change will be and calculate the benefits and costs from the proposer's point of view. The others involved will almost inevitably see the benefits as less and the costs as greater. It is necessary to 'think through' the proposed change and obtain answers to the following questions:

- **Will the change alter job content?**
- **Will it introduce new and unknown tasks?**
- **Will it disrupt established methods of working?**

- Will it rearrange team relationships?
- Will it reduce autonomy or authority?
- Will it be perceived as lowering status?
- Will it lead to job losses?
- Will it result in a loss of pay or other benefits?

On the other side, it is necessary to answer the question: 'What are the benefits in pay, status, job satisfaction and career prospects which are generated by the change as well as the increase in performance?'

Resistance to change may never be overcome completely but it can be reduced through involvement and communications.

Involvement

Involvement in the change process gives people the chance to raise and resolve their concerns and make suggestions about the form of the change and how it should be introduced. The aim is to get 'ownership' – a feeling amongst people that the change is something that they are happy to live with because they have been involved in its planning and introduction – it has become their change.

Communicating plans for change

The first and most critical step for managing change is to develop and communicate a clear image of the future. Resistance and confusion frequently develop because people are unclear about what the future state will be like. Thus the purposes of the change become blurred, and individual expectancies get formed on the basis of incorrect information.

Communications should describe why change is necessary, what the changes will look like, how they will be achieved and how people will be affected by them. The aim is to ensure that unnecessary fears are allayed by keeping people informed using a variety of methods – written communications, the intranet and, best of all, face-to-face briefings and discussions.

10 guidelines for change management

1. The achievement of sustainable change requires strong commitment and visionary leadership.
2. Proposals for change should be based on a convincing business case supported by a practical programme for implementing the change and reaping the benefits.
3. Change is inevitable and necessary. It is necessary to explain why change is essential and how it will affect everyone.
4. Hard evidence and data on the need for change are the most powerful tools for its achievement, but establishing the need for change is easier than deciding how to satisfy it.
5. People support what they help to create. Commitment to change is improved if those affected by change are allowed to participate as fully as possible in planning and implementing it. The aim should be to get them to 'own' the change as something they want and will be glad to live with.
6. Change will always involve failure as well as success. The failures must be expected and learnt from.
7. It is easier to change behaviour by changing processes, structure and systems than to change attitudes.
8. There are always people in organizations who can act as champions of change. They will welcome the challenges and opportunities that change can provide. They are the ones to be chosen as change agents.

9. Resistance to change is inevitable if the individuals concerned feel that they are going to be worse off – implicitly or explicitly. The inept management of change will produce that reaction.

10. Every effort must be made to protect the interests of those affected by change.

12

Handling people problems

If you manage people you have to manage people problems. They are bound to happen and you are the person on the spot who has to handle them. The basic approach you should use in tackling people problems is to:

1. Get the facts. Make sure that you have all the information or evidence you need to understand exactly what the problem is.
2. Weigh and decide. Analyse the facts to identify the causes of the problem. Consider any alternative solutions to the problem and decide which is likely to be the most successful.
3. Take action. Following the decision, plan what you are going to do, establish goals and success criteria and put the plan into effect.
4. Check results. Monitor the implementation of the plan and check.

The most typical problems covered in this chapter are to do with:

- absenteeism;
- disciplinary issues;
- negative behaviour;
- timekeeping;
- under-performance.

Absenteeism

A frequent people problem you probably have to face is that of dealing with absenteeism. A survey by the Chartered Institute of Personnel and Development in 2007 established that absence levels averaged 8.4 days a year per person. Your own organization should have figures which indicate average absence levels. If the levels in your department are below the average for the organization or, in the absence of that information, below the national average, you should not be complacent – you should continue to monitor the absence of individuals to find out whose absence levels are above the average and why. If your department's absence figures are significantly higher than the norm you may have to take more direct action such as discussing with individuals whose absence rates are high the reasons for their absences, especially when it has been self-certificated. You may have to deal with recurrent short-term (one or two days) absence or longer-term sickness absence.

Recurrent short-term absence

Dealing with people who are repeatedly absent for short periods can be difficult to handle. This is because it may be hard to determine when occasional absence becomes a problem or whether it is justifiable, perhaps on medical grounds.

So what do you do about it? Many organizations provide guidelines to managers on the 'trigger points' for action (the amount of absence which needs to be investigated), perhaps based on analyses of the incidence of short-term absence and the level at which it is regarded as acceptable (in many organizations software exists to generate analyses and data which can be made available direct to managers through a self-service system). If guidelines do not exist you can seek advice from an HR specialist, if one is available. In the absence of either of these sources of help and in particularly difficult cases, it may be advisable to recommend to higher management that advice is obtained from an employment law expert.

But this sort of guidance may not be available and you may have to make up your own mind on when to do something and what to do. A day off every other month may not be too serious, although if it happens regularly on a Monday (after weekends in Prague, Barcelona etc?) or a Friday (before such weekends?) you may feel like having a word with the individual, not as a warning but just to let him or her know that you are aware of what is going on. There may be a medical or other acceptable explanation. Return-to-work interviews can provide valuable information. You see the individual and find out why the time was taken off, giving him or her ample opportunity to explain the absence.

In persistent cases of absenteeism you can hold an absence review meeting. Although this would be more comprehensive than a return-to-work interview, it should not at this stage be presented as part of a disciplinary process. The meeting should be positive and constructive. If absence results from a health problem you can find out what the employee is doing about it and if necessary suggest that his or her doctor should be consulted. Or absences may be caused by problems facing a parent or a carer. In such cases you should be sympathetic but you can reasonably discuss with the individual what steps can be taken to reduce the problem, or you might be able to agree on flexible working if that can be arranged. The aim is to get the employee to discuss as openly as possible any factors affecting their attendance and to agree any constructive steps

If after holding an attendance review meeting and, it is to be hoped, agreeing the steps necessary to reduce absenteeism, short-term absence persists without a satisfactory explanation, then another meeting can be held which emphasizes the employee's responsibility for attending work. Depending on the circumstances (each case should be dealt with on its merits), at this meeting you can link any positive support with an indication that following the provision of support you expect absence levels to improve over a defined timescale (an improvement period). If this does not happen, the individual can expect more formal disciplinary action.

Dealing with long-term absence

Dealing with long-term absence can be difficult. The aim should be to facilitate the employee's return to work at the earliest reasonable point while recognizing that in extreme cases the person may not be able to come back. In that case they can fairly be dismissed for lack of capability as long as:

- **the employee has been consulted at all stages;**
- **contact with the employee has been maintained – this is something you can usefully do as long as you do not appear to be pressing them to return to work before they are ready;**
- **appropriate medical advice has been sought from the employee's own doctor, but the employee's consent is needed and employees have the right to see the report and it may be desirable to obtain a second opinion;**
- **all reasonable options for alternative employment have been reviewed as well as any other means of facilitating a return to work.**

The decision to dismiss should only be taken if these conditions are satisfied. It is a tricky one and you should seek advice before taking it, from HR, if available, or from an employment law expert.

Disciplinary issues

Employees can be dismissed because they are not capable of doing the work or for misconduct. It is normal to go through a formal disciplinary procedure containing staged warnings, but instant dismissal can be justified for gross misconduct (eg serious theft) which should preferably be defined in the company's disciplinary procedure or employee handbook. But anyone with a year's service or more can claim unfair dismissal if their employer cannot show that one of these reasons applied, if the dismissal was not reasonable in the circumstances, if a constructive dismissal has taken place, or if there has been a breach of a customary or agreed redundancy procedure and there are no valid reasons for departing from that procedure.

Even if the employer can show to an employment tribunal that there was good reason to dismiss the employee, the tribunal will still have to decide whether or not the employer acted in a reasonable way at the time of dismissal. The principles defining 'reasonable' behaviour are in line with the principles of natural justice and are as follows:

- **The employee should be informed of the nature of the complaint.**
- **The employee should be given the chance to explain.**
- **The employee should be given the opportunity to improve, except in particularly gross cases of incapability or misconduct.**
- **The employee should be warned of the consequences in the shape of dismissal if specified improvements do not take place.**
- **The employer's decision to dismiss should be based on sufficient evidence.**
- **The employer should take any mitigating circumstances into account.**
- **The offence or misbehaviour should merit the penalty of dismissal rather than some lesser penalty.**

Your organization may have a statutory disciplinary procedure. You need to know what that procedure is and the part you are expected to play in implementing it. Whether or not there is a formal procedure, if you believe that disciplinary action is necessary you need you take the following steps when planning and conducting a disciplinary interview:

1. Get all the facts in advance, including statements from people involved.
2. Invite the employee to the meeting in writing, explaining why it is being held and that they have the right to have someone present at the meeting on their behalf.
3. Ensure that the employee has reasonable notice (ideally at least two days).
4. Plan how you will conduct the meeting.
5. Line up another member of management to attend the meeting with you to take notes (they can be important if there is an appeal) and generally provide support.
6. Start the interview by stating the complaint to the employee and referring to the evidence.
7. Give the employee plenty of time to respond and state their case.
8. Take a break as required to consider the points raised and to relieve any pressure taking place in the meeting.
9. Consider what action is appropriate, if any. Actions should be staged, starting with a recorded written warning, followed, if the problem continues, by a first written warning, then a final written warning and lastly, if the earlier stages have been exhausted, disciplinary action, which would be dismissal in serious cases.
10. Deliver the decision, explaining why it has been taken and confirm it in writing.

If all the stages in the disciplinary procedure have been completed and the employee has to be dismissed, or where immediate dismissal can be justified on the grounds of gross misconduct, you may have to carry out the unpleasant duty of dismissing the employee. Again, you should have a colleague or someone from HR with you when you do this. You should:

- **if possible, meet when the office is quiet, preferably on a Friday;**
- **keep the meeting formal and organized;**
- **write down what you are going to say in advance, giving the reason and getting your facts, dates and figures right;**
- **be polite but firm – read out what you have written down and make it clear that it is not open for discussion;**
- **ensure that the employee clears his or her desk and has no opportunity to take away confidential material or use their computer;**
- **see the employee off the premises – some companies use security guards as escorts but this is rather heavy handed, although it might be useful to have someone on call in case of difficulties.**

Handling negative behaviour

You may well come across negative behaviour from time to time on the part of one of the members of your team. This may take the form of lack of interest in the work, unwillingness to cooperate with you or other members of the team, unreasonably complaining about the work or working conditions, grumbling at being asked to carry out a perfectly reasonable task, objecting strongly to being asked to do something extra (or even refusing to do it) – 'it's not in my job description', or, in extreme cases, insolence. People exhibiting negative behaviour may be quietly resentful rather than openly disruptive. They mutter away in the background at meetings and lack enthusiasm.

As a manager you can tolerate a certain amount of negative behaviour as long as the individual works reasonably well and does not upset other team members. You have simply to say to yourself 'It takes all sorts...' and put up with it, although you might quietly say during a review meeting 'You're doing a good job but...'. If, however, you do take this line you have to be specific. You must cite actual instances. It is no good making generalized accusations which will either be openly refuted or internalized by the receiver, making him or her even more resentful.

If the negative behaviour means that the individual's contribution is not acceptable and is disruptive then you must take action. Negative people can be quiet but they are usually angry about something; their negative behaviour is an easy way of expressing their anger. To deal with the problem it is necessary to find out what has made the person angry.

Causes of negative behaviour

There are many possible causes of negative behaviour, which could include one or more of the following:

- a real or imagined slight from you or a colleague;
- a feeling of being put upon;
- a belief that the contribution made by the person is neither appreciated nor rewarded properly in terms of pay or promotion;
- resentment at what was perceived to be unfair criticism;
- anger directed at the company or you because what was considered to be a reasonable request was turned down, eg for leave or a transfer, or because of an unfair accusation.

Dealing with the problem

It is because there can be such a variety of real or imagined causes of negative behaviour that dealing with it becomes one of the most difficult tasks you have to undertake. If the action taken is crude or insensitive the negative behaviour will only be intensified. This might end up in your having to invoke the disciplinary procedure, which should be your last resort.

In one sense, it is easier to deal with an actual example of negative behaviour. This can be handled on the spot. If the problem is one of general attitude rather than specific actions it is more difficult to cope with. Hard evidence may not be sufficiently available. When individuals are accused of being, for example, generally unenthusiastic or uncooperative, they can simply go into denial, and accuse you of being prejudiced. Their negative behaviour may be reinforced.

If you have to deal with this sort of problem it is best to do it informally, either when it arises or at any point during the year when you feel that something has to be done about it. An annual formal performance review or appraisal meeting is not the right time, especially if it produces ratings which are linked to a pay increase. Raising the issue then will only put individuals on the defensive and a productive discussion will be impossible.

The discussion may be informal but it should have three clear objectives:

1. To discuss the situation with individuals, the aim being if possible to get them to recognize for themselves that they are behaving negatively. If this cannot be achieved, then the object is to bring to the attention of individuals your belief that their behaviour is unacceptable in certain ways.
2. To establish the reasons for the individuals' negative behaviour so far as this is feasible.
3. To discuss and agree any actions individuals could take to behave more positively, or what you or the organization could do to remove the causes of the behaviour.

Discussing the problem

Start by asking generally how individuals feel about their work.

Do they have any problems in carrying it out? Are they happy with the support they get from you or their colleagues? Are they satisfied that they are pulling their weight to the best of their ability?

You may find that this generalized start provides the basis for the next two stages – identifying the causes and remedies. It is best if individuals are encouraged to identify for themselves that there is a problem. But in many, if not the majority of cases, this is unlikely to happen. Individuals may not recognize that they are behaving negatively or will not be prepared to admit it.

You will then have to discuss the problem. You could say truthfully that you are concerned because they seem to be unhappy and you wish to know if they feel that you or the organization is treating them unfairly – you want to try to put things right. Give them time to say their piece and then provide a rational response, dealing with specific grievances. If they are not satisfied with your explanation you can say that they will be given the opportunity to discuss the problem with a more senior manager, thus indicating that you recognize that your judgement is not final.

If the response you get to these initial points does not bring out into the open the problem as you see it, you have to explain how the individual's behaviour gives the impression of being negative. Be as specific as possible about the behaviour, bringing up actual instances. For example, a discussion could be based on the following questions: 'Do you recall yesterday's team meeting?', 'How did you think it went?', 'How helpful do you think you were in dealing with the problem?', 'Do you remember saying...?', 'How helpful do you think that remark was?', 'Would it surprise you to learn that I felt you had not been particularly helpful in the following ways...?'

Of course, even if this careful approach is adopted, there will be occasions when individuals refuse to admit that there is anything wrong with their behaviour. If you reach this impasse, then you have no alternative but to spell out to them your perceptions of where they have gone wrong. But do this in a positive way: 'Then I think that it is only fair for me to point out to you that your contribution (to the meeting) would have been more helpful if you had...'

Establishing causes

If the negative behaviour is because of a real or imagined grievance about what you or colleagues or the organization has done, then you have to get individuals to spell this out as precisely as possible. At this point, your job is to listen, not to judge. People can be just as angry about imaginary as real slights. You have to find out how they perceive the problem before you can deal with it.

It may emerge during the discussion that the problem has nothing to do with you or the company. It may be family troubles or worries about health or finance. If this is the case you can be sympathetic and may be able to suggest remedies in the form of counselling or practical advice from within or outside the organization.

If the perceived problem is you, colleagues or the organization, try to get chapter and verse on what it is so that you are in a position to take remedial action or to explain the real facts of the case.

Taking remedial action

If the problem rests with the individual, the objective is, of course, to get them to recognize for themselves that corrective action is necessary and what they need to do about it – with your help as necessary. In this situation you might suggest counselling or recommend a source of advice. But be careful, you don't want to imply that there is something wrong with them. You should go no further than suggesting that individuals may find this helpful – they don't need it but they could benefit from it. You should be careful about offering counselling advice yourself. This is better done by professional counsellors.

If there is anything specific that the parties involved in the situation can do, then the line to take is that we can tackle this problem together: 'This is what I will do', 'This is what the company will do', 'What do you think you should do?' If there is no response to the last question, then this is the point where you have to spell out the action you think they need to take. Be as specific as possible and try to express your wishes as suggestions, not commands. A joint problem-solving approach is always best.

10 approaches to managing negative behaviour

1. Define the type of negative behaviour which is being exhibited. Make notes of examples.
2. Discuss the behaviour with the individual as soon as possible, aiming to get agreement about what it is and the impact it makes.
3. If agreement is not obtained, give actual examples of behaviour and explain why you believe them to be negative.
4. Discuss and so far as possible agree reasons for the negative behaviour, including those attributed to the individual, yourself and the organization.
5. Discuss and agree possible remedies – actions on the part of the individual, yourself or the organization.
6. Monitor the actions taken and the results obtained.
7. If improvement is not achieved and the negative behaviour is significantly affecting the performance of the individual and the team, then invoke the disciplinary procedure.
8. Start with a verbal warning, indicating the ways in which behaviour must improve and give a timescale and offers of further support and help as required.

9. If there is no improvement, issue a formal warning, setting out as specifically as possible what must be achieved over a defined period of time, indicating the disciplinary action that could be taken.
10. If the negative behaviour persists and continues seriously to affect performance, take the disciplinary action.

Handling poor timekeeping

If you are faced with persistent lateness and your informal warnings to the individual concerned seem to have little effect, you may be forced to invoke the disciplinary procedure. If timekeeping does not improve, this could go through the successive stages of a recorded oral warning, a written warning and a final written warning. If the final warning does not work, disciplinary action would have to be taken; in serious cases this would mean dismissal.

Note that this raises the difficult question of time limits when you give a final warning that timekeeping must improve by a certain date, the improvement period. If it does improve by that date and the slate is wiped clean, it might be assumed that the disciplinary procedure starts again from scratch if timekeeping deteriorates again. But it is in the nature of things that some people cannot sustain efforts to get to work on time for long, and deterioration often occurs. In these circumstances, do you have to keep on going through the warning cycles time after time? The answer ought to be no, and the best approach seems to be to avoid stating a finite end date to a final warning period, which implies a 'wipe the slate clean' approach. Instead, the warning should simply say that timekeeping performance will be reviewed on a stated date. If it has not improved, disciplinary action can be taken. If it has, no action will be taken, but the employee is warned that further deterioration will make him or her liable to disciplinary action which may well speed up the normal procedure, perhaps by only using the final warning stage and by reducing the elapsed time between the warning and the review date. There will come a time, if poor timekeeping persists, when you can say 'enough is enough' and initiate disciplinary action.

Dealing with under-performers

You may possibly have someone who is under-performing in your team. If so, what can you do about it? Essentially, you have to spot that there is a problem, understand the cause of the problem, decide on a remedy and make the remedy work.

Poor performance can be the fault of the individual but it could arise because of poor leadership or problems in the system of work. In the case of an individual the reason may be that he or she:

- **could not do it – ability;**
- **did not know how to do it – skill; or**
- **would not do it – attitude;**
- **did not fully understand what was expected of them.**

Inadequate leadership from managers can be the cause of poor performance from individuals. It is the manager's responsibility to specify the results expected and the levels of skill and competence required. As likely as not, when people do not understand what they have to do, it is their manager who is to blame.

Performance can also be affected by the system of work. If this is badly planned and organized or does not function well, individuals cannot be blamed for the poor performance that results. This is the fault of management and they must put it right.

If inadequate individual performance cannot be attributed to poor leadership or the system of work, these are the seven steps you can take to deal with under-performers:

A 7-step approach to managing under-performance

1. Identify the areas of under-performance – be specific.
2. Establish the causes of poor performance.
3. Agree on the action required.
4. Ensure that the necessary support (coaching, training, extra resources etc) is provided to ensure the action is successful.
5. Monitor progress and provide feedback.
6. Provide additional guidance as required.
7. As a last resort, invoke the capability or disciplinary procedure, starting with an informal warning.

References

Adair, J (1973) *The Action-Centred Leader*, McGraw-Hill, London
Bennis, W G and Thomas, R J (2002) *Geeks and Geezers: How Era, Values and Defining Moments Shape Leaders*, Harvard University Press, Boston, MA
Drucker, P (1962) *The Effective Executive*, Heinemann, London
Goleman, D (2001) What makes a leader?, in *What Makes a Leader*, Harvard Business School Press, Boston, MA
Gross, S E (1995) *Compensation for Teams*, Hay, New York
Handy, C (1994) *The Empty Raincoat*, Hutchinson, London
Harvey-Jones, J (1984) *Making it Happen*, Collins, Glasgow
Herzberg, F W, Mausner, B and Snyderman, B (1957) *The Motivation to Work*, Wiley, New York
Industrial Society (1997) Leadership – Steering a New Course, London
Jaques, E (1961) *Equitable Payment*, Heinemann, London
Katzenbach, J and Smith, D (1993) *The Magic of Teams*, Harvard Business School Press, Boston, MA
Kelley, R E (1991) In praise of followers, in *Managing People and Organizations*, ed J Gabarro, Harvard Business School Publications, Boston, MA

Kotter, J P (1991) Power, dependence and effective management, in *Managing People and Organizations*, ed J Gabarro, Harvard Business School Publications, Boston, MA

Latham, G and Locke, R (1979) Goal setting – a motivational technique that works, *Organizational Dynamics*, Autumn, pp 68–80

Maslow, A (1954) *Motivation and Personality*, Harper & Row, New York

McClelland, D C (1961) *The Achieving Society*, Van Norstrand, New York

McGregor, D (1960) *The Human Side of Enterprise*, McGraw-Hill, New York

Pedler, M, Boydell, T and Burgoyne, J (1986) *A Manager's Guide to Self-development*, McGraw-Hill, Maidenhead

Pfeffer, J (1998) Six dangerous myths about pay, *Harvard Business Review*, May/June, pp 109–19

Porter, L and Lawler, E E (1968) *Management Attitudes and Behaviour*, Irwin-Dorsey, Homewood, IL

Thurley, K (1979) *Supervision: A reappraisal*, Heinemann, London

Welch, J (2007) Mindset of a leader, *Leadership Excellence*, 24 (1), pp 8–9

Woodward, J (1968) Resistance to change, *Management International Review*, 8, pp 78–93

Index